ALWAYS FAITHFUL

ALWAYS FAITHFUL

A Memoir of the
Marine Dogs of WWII

★ ★ ★

★ ★ ★

Captain William W. Putney
D. V. M., USMC (RET.)

**Potomac
Books**

Library of Congress Cataloging-in-Publication Data

Putney, William W., 1920–
   Always faithful : a memoir of the Marine dogs of WWII / William W. Putney.—1st ed.
      p. cm.
   Originally published: New York : Free Press, © 2001.
   ISBN 978-1-57488-719-8   (pbk. : alk. paper)
   1. Putney, William W., 1920– 2. World War, 1939–1945—Personal narratives, American. 3. World War, 1939–1945—Campaigns—Guam. 4. United States. Marine Corps. War Dog Platoon, 3rd.—History. 5. Dogs—War use. 6. Veterinarians—United States—Biography. I. Title.
   D767.99.G8P87   2003
   940.54′8173—dc21   2003011326

Potomac Books
22841 Quicksilver Drive
Dulles, Virginia 20166

First Edition

10 9 8 7 6 5 4 3

Praise for William W. Putney's *ALWAYS FAITHFUL*

"In a style reminiscent of James Herriot's *All Creatures Great and Small*, Bill Putney reconstructs his World War II experiences with Marine war dogs, in camp and in the Pacific, as a platoon leader and veterinarian. The result is a fascinating and poignant story."

— **Brigadier General Edwin Howard Simmons,**
USMC (Ret.), Director Emeritus, Marine
Corps History, and author of
Dog Company Six

"Captain Putney's heartfelt documentary of our military canines is a tribute to the animals that have spent their lives protecting American soldiers, and to the men who depended on them to protect America."

— **Congressman Elton Gallegly**
(23rd District, CA)

"Dr. William W. Putney brings an unusual degree of realistic empathy to his account of the training of Marine war dogs and their employment in the recapture of Guam, 1944. There is no Disneyesque artifice in his account of the service of his brave dogs and their Marine handlers. Dr. Putney makes an especially important point that well-trained and adjusted war dogs can return to civil life just like their human counterparts. His expert arguments on war dog training are persuasive."

— **Allan Millett,** author of *Semper Fidelis:*
A History of the United States Marine Corps

"*Always Faithful* is a moving story of the men and the dogs of the Marine War Dog Platoons that contributed so greatly to the successes achieved by the U. S. Marines in the island-hopping battle campaigns against Japanese forces in the Pacific Theater during World War II."

— **Leonard F. Seda**, D. V. M., President,
American Veterinary Medical Association

"*Always Faithful* is like opening a vault to history's secrets. The book yields the tastes, smells, noises, sights, and emotions of the Marine Corps dog handlers during World War II. Dr. Putney's is a riveting account that brings together military and dog history in an unforgettable way and reaffirms the bonds that we keep with our four-legged friends."

— **Michael G. Lemish**, author of *War Dogs: A History of Loyalty and Heroism*

"A great book telling the untold story of the Marine 'Devil Dogs.' It should be of interest to all readers—and especially animal lovers."

— **Captain Arthur J. Haggerty**, former C.O. of the U. S. Army K-9 Corps and author of *How to Teach Your Dog to Talk*

"The canines who gave selflessly to protect our boys in the Pacific is one of the great untold stories of World War II—until now. A compelling read, *Always Faithful* is sure to touch the heart of anyone who has ever loved a dog."

— **Mary Elizabeth Thurston**, author of *The Lost History of the Canine Race*

"Bill Putney's accounts of war dog training conducted at Camp Lejeune through the employment of those dogs in the Pacific Island Campaigns depict what can only be termed a 'true success.' The exploits of Putney's dogs and Marines truly lived up to our Corps motto: Semper Fidelis—Always Faithful."

— **Colonel Barney Barnum**, President of the Medal of Honor Society and recipient of the Medal of Honor for actions in Vietnam

★　★　★

CONTENTS

PROLOGUE

Less than twenty-four hours after the attack on Pearl Harbor, the Japanese invaded Guam, an American possession. The small Pacific island, virtually defenseless, held out for only four days. For the next two and a half years, the brave people of Guam endured a horrible occupation: they were starved, beaten, and herded into concentration camps. Many of Guam's people were summarily shot for crimes they did not commit. Some were beheaded. No other American civilians suffered so much under so brutal a conqueror.

On July 21, 1944, the Americans struck back. The battle for Guam lasted only a few weeks, until August 10, 1944, when the island was declared secured. In those weeks, American Marine, Army, and Navy casualties exceeded 7,000. An estimated 18,500 Japanese were killed, and another 8,000 Japanese remained hidden in the jungle refusing to surrender.

Among our dead were 25 dogs, specially trained by the U.S. Marines to search out the enemy hiding in the bush, detect mines and booby traps, alert troops in foxholes at night to approaching Japanese, and to carry messages, ammunition and medical supplies. They were buried in a small section of the Marine Cemetery, in a rice paddy on the landing beach at Asan that became known as the War Dog Cemetery.

I was the commanding officer of the 3rd War Dog Platoon during the battle for Guam. Lieutenant William T. Taylor and I led 110 men and 72 dogs through training, first at Camp Lejeune, North Carolina; then at Camp Pendleton, California; later on Guadalcanal and then into battle on Guam.

Most of the young Marines were assigned to the war dog program only by a twist of fate. Some had never owned a dog in their lives, and some were even afraid of them. But trained as dog handlers, they were expected to scout far forward of our lines, in treacherous jungle terrain, searching for Japanese soldiers hidden in caves or impenetrable thickets. Under these circumstances, the rifles we carried were often useless; a handler's most reliable weapons were his dog's highly developed senses of smell and hearing, which could alert him far in advance of an enemy ambush or attack, or the presence of a deadly mine, so he could warn in turn the Marines who followed behind at a safer distance. It was one of the most dangerous jobs in World War II, and more dogs were employed by the 2nd and 3rd Platoons on Guam than in all of the other battles in the Pacific.

During the course of the war, 15 of the handlers in the 2nd and 3rd Platoons were killed: 3 at Guam, 4 on Saipan and 8 on Iwo Jima. These men were among the bravest and best-trained Marines of World War II, and were awarded the medals to prove it. During the course of some of the war's most vicious battles—Guam, Saipan, Iwo Jima and Okinawa—they were awarded five Silver Stars and seven Bronze Stars for heroism in action, and more than forty Purple Hearts for wounds received in battle.

In these battles, as in their training, the men learned to depend on their dogs and to trust their dogs' instincts with their lives. Yet when I returned home from overseas, I found that rather than spend the time and expense to detrain the dogs, our military had begun to destroy them. Our dogs, primarily Doberman Pinschers and German Shepherds, had been recruited from the civilian population with the promise that they be returned, intact, when the war ended. Now, however, higher-ups argued that these dogs suffered from the "junkyard dog" syndrome: they were killers. Higher-ups were wrong. I lobbied for the right to detrain these dogs and won. Our program of deindoctrination was overwhelmingly successful: out of the 549 dogs that returned from the war, only 4 could not be detrained and returned to civilian life. Household pets once, the dogs became household pets again. In many cases, in fact, because the original, civilian owners were unable or unwilling to take the dogs back, the dogs went home with the handlers that they had served so well during the war.

★　★　★

More than fifty years have passed since the Battle of Guam. The dogs, of course, are long gone, and to the annual reunions fewer and fewer veterans of the war dog platoons return. Although it was a small chapter in the history of that worldwide conflagration, the story of the war dog platoons is significant. The dogs proved so valuable on Guam that every Marine division was assigned a war dog platoon and they paved the way for the many dogs that have followed them in the armed services, most famously in Vietnam.

For their contribution to the war effort, the dogs paid a dear price, but the good they did was still far out of proportion to the sacrifice they made. They and their handlers led over 550 patrols on Guam alone, and encountered enemy soldiers on over half of them, but were never once ambushed. They saved hundreds of lives, including my own.

This book is dedicated to the memory of those loving, courageous and faithful dogs of the 2nd and 3rd War Dog Platoons. They embodied the Marine Corps motto, Semper Fidelis.

Rest in peace, dear ones.

WILLIAM W. PUTNEY, D.V.M., CAPTAIN, USMC (RET.)
WOODLAND HILLS, CALIFORNIA

CHAPTER ONE

CAMP LEJEUNE, NORTH CAROLINA

On the night of July 25, 1944, 7,500 Japanese sat atop Mt.
Tenjo, on the island of Guam, steeling themselves in prepara-
tion for a banzai attack on F Company of the 9th Marines, en-
trenched in the foothills below them. I was one of those
Marines. With my men I waited in trepidation in the stillness
that preceded the assault. Past experience told us that these as-
saults came with a sudden fury, unpredictable, out of the night.

But this time we had an advantage. Pfc. Ed Adamski and
his Doberman, Big Boy, were stationed in a forward outpost. At
10 P.M. Big Boy leaped up, his sensitive nose pointed directly at
Mt. Tenjo. The attack was on.

I had arrived at the War Dog Training School at Camp Lejeune,
North Carolina, about one year before: on June 1, 1943, twenty-
three years old and fresh out of veterinary school. I had grown up on
a farm in Virginia, and although I attended Virginia Polytechnic Institute as a mechanical engineering student, a job in the veterinary
medical lab on the agriculture campus changed my mind about
what I wanted to do. Until then, I had never met a bona fide veterinarian; where I came from, veterinary medicine was most often dis-

pensed by a local farmer or butcher. But that part-time job convinced me to transfer to Auburn University to study to be a vet.

Despite my education, I had not joined the Marines to care for animals or to inspect meat and eggs—tasks then normally delegated to anyone with a veterinarian's degree. I had been reared in the southern tradition that serving in the military of one's country during war was an honor and the ultimate test of mettle. In 1937, at age seventeen, I had joined Company G of the 116th Infantry of the 29th Infantry Division and served as a private through 1939. But I was determined to become a line officer—a fighting, or combat, officer as opposed to either an enlisted man or a service, or specialist, officer—and went back to school at Auburn, where I joined the field artillery ROTC.

Upon graduation, I was accepted into the Marine Corps and sworn in as a second lieutenant in the United States Marine Corps Reserve on February 9, 1943. Almost immediately, I was ordered to the 24th Reserve Officers' Class at Quantico, Virginia, for three months of infantry training. I expected to continue training at the advanced artillery school, but it was not to be. My initial orders were recalled, and I was ordered instead to the War Dog Training School, at Camp Lejeune. The new school, it seemed, needed a line officer. Someone must have thought that with my veterinary degree I would be a natural.

Colonel Clifton Cates, Commandant of the Marine Corps Schools at Quantico, briefed me on my assignment. Some years earlier, General Augusto Sandino's bandits in Nicaragua had victimized the Marines by grabbing any available dogs and tying them around their camp for security. If a Marine patrol approached, the dogs barked, tipping off the bandits. By the time the Marines arrived, the bandits had fled, leaving behind only smoldering fires and occasionally a pot of still warm beans.

In the recent battle for Guadalcanal, the colonel said, the Japanese had ruled the nighttime jungle, infiltrating the Marine lines and killing Marines while they slept in their foxholes. The Marine Corps decided that if it could train dogs to alert without barking to an approaching enemy, the Americans could turn the tables on the Japanese. My veterinary education was not mentioned; the War Dog Training School had requested a line officer and I was it.

So here I was, and I could tell from the sign at the entrance that my veterinary skills might come in handy. It read U.S. MARINES—CAMP LEJEUNE, N.C.—WAR DOG TRAINING COMPANY. But the image of the dog painted beneath the lettering was clearly that of a Great Dane, not a Doberman Pinscher, the official war dog of the Marine Corps. Had nobody noticed the mistake?

★ ★ ★

In 1943, Camp Lejeune was still woodsy and undeveloped. Part pine forest, part farmland before the Marines took over, there were still corn rows here and there. In places, purple grapes known as muscadines grew wild into the tops of trees. The war dog training camp, originally a Civilian Conservation Corps camp established in the 1930s, sat on a bluff overlooking the north fork of the New River. Except for the dog camp and Montford Point, home of the black Marines (in those days the Marine Corps was still segregated), all units were located on the other side of the river. Camp Lejeune might have been described either as a paradise—the piece of land jutting out into the river across from the dog camp was actually named Paradise Point—or a swampy, insect-infested hellhole, depending on what you were doing at the time.

Captain Jackson H. Boyd welcomed me to camp. He was fifty-two years old, more than six feet tall and still slender. He'd served as a battery commander in World War I and had been wounded in the Battle of Argonne Forest. Between the wars, he had worked as a stockbroker in Southern Pines, North Carolina, where he was master of the hounds for the Southern Pines Hunt Club. More important, he was genuinely glad to see me. The school had not yet had a single line officer, so Boyd had petitioned headquarters for one and I was the result. He knew that I was a veterinarian but said my purpose would be to train two platoons in infantry tactics and eventually to command one overseas. He assured me that my gunnery sergeant, Lawrence Holdren, a sixteen-year veteran with duty in Haiti, Nicaragua and China, would be able to provide plenty of experience and advice.

In the War Dog Training School both men and dogs would be trained for combat. There were to be three basic functions for the dogs. Scout dogs would be trained to scout in front of the infantry in advances and on patrols, guard prisoners, provide night security in foxholes and outposts, and enter caves and pillboxes to determine whether enemy was present. Messenger dogs would carry messages between their two handlers as well as small amounts of ammunition, medicine and other supplies in saddlebags to units that could not be reached otherwise because of enemy fire. Mine dogs would be taught to detect mines, trip wires, booby traps and other explosive devices buried or hidden from view. The handlers, too, would learn a variety of skills. The handlers of the scout dogs, for example, would be trained as expert infantry scouts: they would learn how to trail men through the forest or jungle and be schooled in all aspects of small arms. But what was most important was that the handlers learn their dogs.

The use of animals—from homing pigeons to horses—in war was nothing new: thousands of years ago, Greek and Roman soldiers had sent dogs with spiked collars into battle. In the American Civil War, a few dogs that accompanied their masters to war were used as sentries and guard dogs. At Andersonville Prison in Georgia, thirteen dogs were used for attacking escaping prisoners, and guard dogs were used at Libby and Castle Thunder Prisons. But there was no official corps of dogs for either the Union or Confederate armies.*

By World War I, dogs were being used by the thousands by all combatants. Red Cross dogs were used to find wounded men in No Man's Land, the ground separating the lines of the combatants. A dog brought back a helmet or some article of clothing to his line and then led rescue squads to retrieve the wounded man. (Today there is a monument to the Red Cross dogs of World War I at the Hartsdale Pet Cemetery in Hartsdale, New York.) Messenger dogs were used extensively as were dogs to pull carts with supplies and equipment, and there is a statue in Brussels of a dog pulling a machine gun on a cart for soldiers moving to the front.

Unaccountably, during World War II the Marines did not consider using dogs until after Guadalcanal, where canines, with their extraordinary sense of smell, could conceivably provide an excellent defense against the night infiltration by the Japanese.

Before I arrived, the 1st War Dog Platoon had already been sent on its way. But there were problems. The Corps had recruited a

---

*This information is taken from Michael G. Lemish's *War Dogs: A History of Loyalty and Heroism.*

schoolteacher as commanding officer for the first platoon because he was an amateur dog trainer, but he had no military training. By the time I had arrived in Lejeune, they had moved on to Camp Pendleton, California, where Carl Spitz, a professional dog trainer and German soldier in World War I, had been hired to complete the dog training before they were sent overseas.

Captain Boyd pulled a piece of paper from his shirt pocket and handed it to me. It was a memo, addressed to all personnel of the War Dog Training School, and it outlined the spirit in which Marine handlers and their dogs would be trained and cared for. It read, in part, as follows:

> The handler will learn that the dog will be loyal and can be depended upon. It can be expected that the man and his dog will create a team that will be unbreakable. The handler in this course will develop a feeling of pride, companionship and ownership in his own dog by the natural response of one to the other.
>
> To further accomplish this, the handler will furnish all care and maintenance of his charge. He will feed and water his dog on a scheduled basis. He will clean and groom his dog every day as directed by his instructors. He will maintain his animal's quarters in a manner specified by the Veterinarian.
>
> Training will consist of the following exercises to teach the dog to heel, sit, down, stay, come (on recall), crawl, and jump both high and broad. These exercises will be taught using both voice commands and arm and hand signals.

The method used shall be one of reward for accomplishment. This shall be a combination of voice praise, physical petting and fondling. Under no circumstances will physical punishment or abuse be tolerated. Reprimands shall be restricted to oral disapproval. Any violations will be severely dealt with.

Training, according to the memo, would be completed by July 15, 1943.

★ ★ ★

I would be commanding both the 2nd and 3rd Platoons until a second officer arrived to take charge of one of them, and thus was not expected to be responsible for the dogs' health. The chief veterinarian, First Lieutenant James A. B. Stewart, had that job, and, as I learned the first night at chow, he managed to make the most of it. Five minutes after we sat down to eat in the mess hall, Stewart, a roly-poly man whose lopsided face looked like his mother had laid him too long on one side, whispered a warning and an invitation.

"Don't eat much of this stuff. It'll kill you. Come over to the dog hospital and I'll give you a good meal."

A few minutes later, he made a great show of pushing his plate away and announcing to Captain Boyd that he was on a diet. He asked to be excused and said he would take me over to the dog hospital and show me around. Boyd looked at the pudgy vet doubtfully but excused us. As we walked toward the dog hospital, a lone building near the river, he asked why I was in the Marine Corps as a line officer—implying that I must be nuts.

I told him that I didn't want to puddle guts in the Veterinary Corps of the Army, so when the Marine Corps offered a real commission to me as an ROTC grad, I took it.

"It's your funeral," he said. "This is as far forward as I intend to go."

I could see why. Inside the hospital Stewart pulled two large steaks from the refrigerator, plopped them onto a broiler pan and pushed them into the oven. He plucked two steaming baked potatoes from the oven and set the stove on broil. He got first-rate sides of beef from the commissary for the dogs, he explained. "I inspect it by ripping out the tenderloin and broiling it here. It always passes."

He sliced some tomatoes, and in a few minutes we dug into a meal far better than anything I would ever eat in the mess hall. When it was dark, I excused myself and headed for the officers' quarters, where I quickly found my room, unpacked my few things, hung up my uniforms and went to bed. My first meal at Camp Lejeune had rivaled Delmonico's. It seemed like a good start.

The second day began far less peacefully, with a squawking, screeching sound that blared in a certain, vaguely identifiable rhythm. It was reveille all right, but the worst version I had ever heard. It succeeded in its mission: nobody could sleep through it. As I finished dressing, someone knocked at the door. I opened it to find a tall, thin, sandy-haired Marine wearing sergeant's stripes on his neatly pressed fatigues. He introduced himself as Sergeant Raymond Barnowsky. "Everybody calls me Barney," he said, handing me a roster of troops.

I asked him where he got the field music.

"Oh, that's Spielman. We had a bugle but no field music. Spielman said he played bugle in the Cub Scouts, so we recruited him."

Outside, men were tumbling out of barracks, grabbing at bits of clothing, tugging at shoelaces, and squaring away caps. When the men had lined up, Barnowsky screamed at them to get back into the barracks. "When I blow this whistle, I want you men to break those doors down getting out here! I'm giving you sixty seconds."

The men scampered back into the barracks, and when Barnowsky blew his whistle, they came running, falling, knocking into each other and scrambling toward their assigned places. Barnowsky called them to attention and looked at his watch. It had taken sixty-two seconds. It was Barnowsky, trained at the Army dog training facility at Fort Robinson, Nebraska, who had the major responsibility for training the men and dogs. He dressed the ranks, walking from one end to the other, then tapped one Marine on the shoulder with his swagger stick.

"Stand over there. I'll get to you later."

The Marine moved out of ranks. His dungarees were dirty and wrinkled. His hair was scruffy and hung over his forehead, protruding from a crumpled cap that sat sideways on top of his head. He was about five feet ten, but stocky and powerfully built. He had one shoe in his hand and the other on his foot, the laces loose and untied. The look on his face was one of total despair.

The troops of A and B Barracks, like the ragged Marine out of ranks, looked like kids, which they were. Most were teenagers. A few were older, but not many. Just out of boot camp, they looked skinny and weak, and bore little resemblance to the tough, confident Marines on recruiting posters. Barnowsky returned to the front of the formation, saluted, and said, "Ready for roll call, sir."

I looked at the roster and noticed that the names were so foreign to me that I feared I would never learn how to pronounce them. In desperation, I handed the roster back to Barnowsky and yelled loudly, "Sergeant, call the roll!"

I listened carefully as each name was called. Occasionally, there was a familiar Irish, Scottish, English or Jewish name, but for the most part they were Polish or Italian. I eventually learned how to call the roll, but it took a long time. One Marine's name was Olswfski, pronounced Ol-shev-ski.

"All present and accounted for, sir," said Barnowsky. Then he turned his attention to the Marine he had called from the ranks. He berated him for his sloppiness, then turned to me. "Maybe you'd better have a talk with him." His voice had turned softer and showed genuine concern.

When the men fell in again, Raymond Tomaszewski lagged behind the other men. His fatigues were still a mess. He had his shoes on, but the laces still were not tied, and dragged on the ground. I beckoned to the bedraggled Marine and we headed to the training office. Inside, I asked him what was the matter.

He hesitated, then began. His uncle, it seems, was in the Marines and had told him how great it was. When Raymond's number came up, he chose the Corps and went to boot camp. That was okay. He had expected it to be tough. But he didn't volunteer for this outfit. Some gunny sergeant had pointed his swagger stick at him and said, "You just volunteered for the dog outfit."

He lowered his head. "Sir, I ain't ever had a dog in my life. I just don't feel right talking to a dog. Makes me nervous."

But the problem was not so much a lack of expertise as a lack of pride. Tomaszewski, or Ski, as we came to call him, had been a high-school football star who had dreamed of being a Marine and whose vision of the Corps was every bit as romantic as mine. Now he was talking to dogs instead of killing Japanese, and he was ashamed. The question of respectability was one that I would face with many of the men in my platoon and outside of it and, at first, within myself as well. I loved animals, of course, but I had not come to the Marines for them. My veterinarian's license was, at the moment, unwanted expertise: it had relegated me to the ignominy of the dog corps.

While I thought about the morale of my men, Stewart, working on a dog nearby, called out to Ski, "Give me a hand with Sparky. I've got to probe his foot and I need some muscle."

A large Doberman was lying on his side on the examination table, his handler off to one side, one hand on the dog's shoulder, the other clamping the dog's mouth shut. Tomaszewski stepped forward, put his right elbow on the dog's shoulder and grasped both front paws with his right hand. He placed his left elbow over Sparky's flank and held his rear feet in his left hand.

Stewart took a probe and a pair of forceps from the instrument cabinet and advanced toward Sparky's hind foot. He inserted the forceps into a hole in the footpad and extracted a small stone. Sparky strained, but his entire body was caught in Tomaszewski's vise grip. There wasn't the slightest motion in the foot. Stewart applied a swab of Metaphen to the wound and gave Sparky a pat on the buttocks. Stewart said he had some twenty-five dogs coming in the afternoon. Could Ski lend a hand?

I was impressed at how easily Ski had controlled the big Doberman, rendering the animal absolutely motionless on the examining table. After Ski left, I told the vet that Ski was having a tough time adjusting to being a dog handler. Would Stewart use him as an assistant? It might come in handy when we went overseas to have someone trained as a dog corpsman.

Stewart laughed. "It's fine with me—I like his unmilitary appearance."

I spoke to the top sergeant, who gave it his blessing. From now on Tomaszewski would report to Stewart. For Tomaszewski, his work as a veterinary assistant was the beginning of the pride that he would eventually feel in himself and in the 2nd Platoon. For me it was the beginning of leadership and the start of what would soon become a profound sense of attachment and dedication to the 2nd. I had helped a Marine and in doing so strengthened the whole platoon. I had done a good deed, and it would be repaid manyfold in the jungles of Guam.

★　★　★

Ski was not the only Marine who hadn't volunteered for the war dog detachment—the four-legged Marines hadn't volunteered either. Sergeant Barnowsky had taken nineteen Marines to the Army's dog training facility at Fort Robinson, Nebraska, where he and the men completed a course in dog training. In early February 1943, they returned to Camp Lejeune with forty Army dogs. These dogs, mostly German Shepherds, became the first Marine Corps war dogs.

After this initial acquisition, the Doberman Pinscher Club of America stepped in and persuaded the Corps that club members could provide, for free, all the dogs necessary for the duration of the war. As a consequence, the club became the official recruiter, the Doberman became the official dog, and the president of the club became a powerful influence at Marine Corps headquarters.

The Doberman Pinscher is a relatively new breed, being recognized only in 1900. It was perfected by Ludwig Dobermann of Thuringia. In its ancestry are the Rottweiler, the Black and Tan Terrier, the Smooth-Haired German Pinscher and the Manchester terrier. It is classified by the American Kennel Club as a working dog, measuring twenty-four to twenty-eight inches tall and of very muscular build, often weighing much more than would appear. The Doberman thus has an appearance of nobility. It is sleek and quick, loyal to its master, and devoted to his family. The dog has an excellent nose, and, more important, the heart and spirit of a gentleman—when properly trained.*

But a problem arose right away. Many of the dogs were not well trained. Owners of vicious dogs were certain their dogs were just what the Marine Corps was looking for in a war dog. In fact, the opposite is true. Some aggressiveness is necessary, but it is acceptable only when the handler can control it. More important traits are similar to those that most people value in a hunting dog or household pet: intelligence, tractability, loyalty, stamina, dependability and an acute sense of hearing and smell.

But we learned that even dogs that appeared incorrigible could often be reformed. One such dog was Herman.

One morning as I returned from chow, Stewart called to me across the quadrangle to meet him at the kennels. Would I go into town with him and Ski to receive a shipment of dogs coming from Chicago?

We drove into Jacksonville to meet the train carrying our latest canine recruits. As we pulled into the railroad yard, one of the two Marines who had accompanied the dogs from Chicago waved us over. Everything was shipshape on the trip, he reported, except for one really mean dog. This particular dog was so angry and so tough that every time they took him out to clean his crate they had to use a "come along"—a three-foot pipe with a looped rope at the end that enabled the men to control the dog while keeping him at bay. The Marine warned us to keep our hands away from this dog unless we wanted a bloody stump.

---

*Information taken from *The Complete Dog Book* of the American Kennel Club.

Herman was not hard to find. As Stewart walked down the row of crates containing dogs, a big Doberman suddenly charged the door of its cage, snarling and even biting the bars in frenzy. Stewart jumped back and yelled at the others to stay away. He feared the dog's attacks might have weakened the crate's bars and hinges during the ride from Chicago. If Herman didn't get over his rage, Stewart said, he'd be sent home with a discharge "for the good of the service."

The men began loading the crates and dogs into the trucks. It was an easy job until two Marines picked up Herman's crate. The big dog let out a howl and charged the door again. The Marines dropped the crate and headed to the door, knocking down three others in their great desire to escape to the safety of the outdoors. Stewart broke out in laughter and chided the Marines for their cowardice. But then he stopped and in a serious voice admonished the men to never approach a strange dog with sudden movements. Announce your presence by calling the dog's name, Stewart said, then proceed with confidence.

The two men eyed the veterinarian apprehensively, but gamely approached the crate again. They called out the dog's name and said in reassuring tones that he would not be hurt. But as soon as one of them jiggled the crate, Herman charged again, snarling and howling as before.

"Isn't having much effect on him, Lieutenant," said the nervous Marine.

Stewart said not to worry, just pick up the crate and put it in the truck. Eventually, all the dogs made it into the trucks and back to camp. The crates were unloaded and lined up, and Stewart ordered the men to bring the dogs into the sick bay one at a time with their papers.

One by one, the dogs were given their physicals. Ski lifted each onto the examining table and took its temperature while Stewart opened the envelope containing the dog's papers and health records. Stewart measured each dog's height at its withers, examined his eyes, teeth, coat, legs, feet, heart and lungs. Then he drew urine through a catheter and blood from the dog's right forearm. Spreading a drop on a glass slide, he looked through the microscope. Heartworm was a potential problem because of the large numbers of mosquitoes at Camp Lejeune. "Lots of these dogs are going to get infected," he grumbled. "They should have put this camp someplace else."

After this initial exam, the dogs were kept in quarantine for ten days to watch for incubating diseases. The waiting period helped the dogs to adjust to their new life. Afterward, if they passed our behavioral tests, all their health data would be transferred to a permanent record, and a serial number would be tattooed on the inside of their ear. From then on, they would be Marines.

Finally, it was Herman's turn. For him an exam was out of the question. Herman was still in such a foul temper that Stewart had him taken to the fenced-in quarantine area still in his crate, and used a long rope to open the door latch. When the door swung open, Herman flew out, charging the men standing outside the chain link fence. Frothing at the mouth, fangs exposed, he took one leap, grabbed the fence in his teeth and bit down hard.

Stewart instructed the men to leave Herman alone and under no circumstances to open the gate; water and food were to be pushed under it. Then he ordered Ski to go to the supply shack and draw a padlock. "I'll lock him in myself and keep the key in my pocket." To more effectively illustrate the danger Herman posed, Stewart opened his jacket, exposing his right armpit and the area eight inches below. It looked like a hand grenade had exploded under his arm. In March, a Doberman had gotten him down and Stewart had raised his arm to protect his face. Fortunately, one of the men grabbed a mop with a heavy handle and beat the big dog off of him. It took fifty-seven stitches to close Stewart's wound.

Of the twenty-five dogs examined, four failed to pass and were put in quarantine to await shipment back to their owners. One was rejected because of a generally unthrifty condition and emaciation; one was too small to meet the standards; the third was blind in one eye because of an old injury; and the last showed evidence of a broken leg that had not been set properly, reducing the motion in the knee joint. Stewart looked at the card and noted that the dog had been recruited as a messenger dog. The poor devil could hardly walk, much less run.

Herman didn't get his physical that day or the next or the next— it took a whole week.

The following day, Lieutenant Wilson Davis, a thirty-seven-year-old wholesale produce merchant from Baltimore who had been an amateur dog trainer in civilian life, administered the behavioral test to the other dogs, which consisted of tests for gun-shyness, cowardice aggressiveness, or overaggressiveness. He began by throwing small firecrackers in the vicinity of a dog. If the dog did not try to run or hide behind his handler or begin shaking violently, the size of the explosive was increased. Finally, Davis tossed torpedo bombs, which made a terrific noise and caused some minor concussive damage when they exploded. Meanwhile, the handler walked the dog around the ring on a leash, calling him by name and assuring him that everything was all right. If the dog showed no sign of excessive nervousness, he passed.

Next the dogs were brought into a ring and tethered to a two-foot-long spring that was attached to a wall. To test for aggressiveness, a Marine dressed in a padded suit entered the ring. He approached the dogs with a menacing stance and began beating the ground with a limber switch. Occasionally, he swatted the dog's front leg to see if he could arouse the dog to attack him.

Many would not: one dog was rejected for cowardice—instead of attacking, he crouched behind his handler, whimpering and shaking; another was rejected because he was a fear biter, a very dangerous animal in any situation. In most cases, a fear biter is an outright coward. In this case, the dog gave a good show of courage, at first, but could not suppress all of the telltale signs of cowardice: in a threatening situation his tail was pulled down over his backside and his hind legs were pulled underneath him. When pressed by the agitator, the dog backed up and cowered, but the moment the man turned his back, the dog leaped forward and tried to bite the seat of the man's pants. This kind of dog may be the most dangerous and is often responsible for injuring children and old people. When children cry or scream, these dogs can become hysterical and attack. Finally, one dog was rejected because he was too aggressive. He worked himself into such a frenzy of hysteria during the exercise that he could not be calmed despite his handler's best efforts. He turned on his handler, howling and biting. When the handler retreated to the center of the ring, blood dripping from his left hand, the dog then went after the dog next to him. We sent him home to his lucky family.

In all, seven of the twenty-five dogs received were now rejected, a typical percentage, Stewart said. Throughout the war, 25 to 30 percent of the dogs received at Camp Lejeune were returned because they were unsuitable, and even more would be sent home after the greater test of combat where the lives of the handler, the dog, and the Marines with them depended on an intelligent dog that never lost its cool under any kind of fire.

A week later, Stewart and I went to check on Herman, in the hope that he had settled down. Several Marines were lounging around the quarantine area, and one of them, a man who appeared to be much older than the others, was singing a tune in a foreign language and playing a small concertina with hands almost as large as the squeeze box.

Someone yelled, "Officers on deck," and the men jumped to attention.

As soon as the music stopped, Herman charged the fence, fangs bared, screaming as usual. The concertina player yelled something in a foreign language, and Herman suddenly backed down. He had understood.

The singer's name was Mike Pappas, from Tarpon Springs, Florida, the song, Pappas told Stewart, a Greek lullaby often sung by sponge divers as they sat around their boats after harvesting sponges. He didn't think the song had a real name.

Pappas was older: in fact, he was a "retread," a Marine who had served before and had reenlisted to serve away from the front lines and thus release a younger man for combat duty. The Corps had agreed that when his training at the War Dog School was over, he and his dog would be sent to a defense establishment in the United States as sentries.

Stewart asked Pappas to sing the song again, and as he sang, Herman crawled to the front of the run and lay down with his feet outstretched and his head cocked to listen. Stewart asked Pappas to call Herman in Greek. When he did, Herman sat up, looked at Pappas and then slowly backed away, his eyes glued on the big Marine. Pappas pulled a piece of hard candy that we Marines called "pogie bait" from his pocket. "Come on, boy, here's a treat for you," he said in Greek, "come and get it."

He held out his hand with the candy, but Herman wasn't ready and backed away a little farther. He understood what Pappas was saying but was not yet ready to fully trust him. Too much had happened to him in the last week: he had been taken from his home, thrown into a crate and kept there for days until being placed in a cage surrounded by incomprehensible strangers.

But from that day forward, no one but Pappas was to spend time with Herman. Pappas would feed him, water him and talk to him in Greek. Pappas, too, missed the language of his parents, and he took his instructions seriously. He spent hours with Herman, sang Greek songs to him, coaxed him with soothing Greek phrases, and even cursed him in Greek when Herman ignored him. For the first three days, Pappas made little progress, but any at all was an improvement. Finally, Herman began moving closer to Pappas. At last, on the fourth day, Herman ate his dinner from Pappas's hand. Pappas gritted his teeth and closed his eyes as he let Herman lick the juice off his fist. When he realized that his hand was still intact, he opened his eyes and caught a look on Herman's face that admitted "You got me."

By the fifth day, Herman bounced to the gate when he saw Pappas coming. Pappas opened the padlock, walked into the enclosure and Herman leapt for the feed pan in Mike's hand. Pappas set the food pan on the shipping crate that had been in the run since Herman's arrival, attached the leash to his collar and yelled "Heel" as he had seen the trainers do. Herman followed awkwardly. He was not completely lead-trained, but did appear to have some familiarity with a leash. After ten minutes of walking around the enclosure, Pappas took off the leash and placed the food pan on the ground in front of Herman.

By the sixth day, Pappas and Herman were going for walks around the camp, while the Marines who remembered Herman from his earlier days scattered for cover. The next day, Pappas and Herman climbed the steps and entered the sick bay for Herman's belated examination. He passed with flying colors, and Stewart duly filled out a record book:

HERMAN
War Dog #178

As he was tattooing the identification number into Herman's ear, Stewart commended Pappas for taking only seven days to turn Herman into a good Marine. It had taken God seven days to make the whole world, he reminded Pappas—which might have been easier.

★ CHAPTER TWO ★

TRAINING

There was no rhyme or reason to the process of assigning dogs. No one took into account a particular Marine's experience with dogs—some of the men had never owned one, while others had grown up on farms and knew a lot about dogs. Nor was the dog's personality considered when matching dog and handler. Peppy, a large, aggressive black Doberman, nearly ninety pounds of muscle, was probably the wrong dog for Benny Goldblatt, a skinny nineteen-year-old from New England. On the other hand, Keith Schaible, another wiry nineteen-year-old, was assigned to Butch, a Doberman whose temper was hidden underneath a ring of light beige fur around his mouth that gave the impression that he was always smiling—and perfectly matched the sly grin that lit up Schaible's face. Pal, a Shepherd, and Ben Dickerson, from Alexandria, Virginia, were also made for each other. Cool, lean, and mean, both would soon become any enemy's nightmare.

Some of the men traded the dogs they were assigned, but this was done strictly on the sly. In any event, there was hardly time for the men to discover whether the dogs they had been issued were good matches; basic training was about to begin.

Obedience training came first. A squad consisting of twelve handlers and their dogs were assigned to a trainer. The squad marched to a large field about half a mile from camp, designated the outer training field, as opposed to the drill field located in the camp's center quadrangle. The men and dogs formed a circle on the outer training field with the trainer in the center. The trainer demonstrated the correct position of the dog for each command, beginning with Heel. The men marched around the circle, each dog's shoulder at its handler's left knee as the handler repeatedly commanded "Heel, Heel" followed by the dog's name. At the trainer's command to halt, each handler said "Sit, Sit," and gently urged the dog into a sitting position on his left side. This was repeated over and over again until dogs and handlers responded automatically to the trainer's commands.

Down, Stay, Come and Crawl were added to the repertoire, and once these exercises were mastered using voice commands, the handlers began using arm and hand signals. Controlling the dogs silently would be crucial when moving through enemy territory. Holding the arm above the head with the palm facing the dog meant for the dog to stop. Lowering the arm meant "Down." To bring the dog up to a sitting position, the handler held his arm at his side with his palm in a scooping position facing the dog. The arm extended in front of the handler with the wrist bent backward and the palm facing the dog meant "Stay." Extending the arm horizontally, then rapidly sweeping it down and backward meant for the dog to come. These arm and hand signals were repeated over and over again until the dog responded immediately.

Just as the dogs came to understand what certain voice commands and hand signals meant, they learned, through constant repetition, the significance of the collars that the handlers placed on them. Collars were a vital part of training; choke chain collars were used when drilling, during obedience training and whenever the dog was out of his kennel or attached to a stake and chain. Flat leather collars replaced the choke chain when the dogs were doing tactical training in the field. When the leather collars were placed around their necks, the dogs learned that it was time to work and training rules were in effect. That meant no barking or playing around.

Silence was an absolute necessity if the dogs were to be used in the field. To teach the dog not to bark, the handler held the dog's mouth shut with one hand, and shook his other hand in front of the dog's face admonishing him with a stern "No, no." This was done in circumstances where a dog would naturally bark—for example, when strangers or animals approached. Gradually, the dog understood that when the leather collar was on, barking was not allowed, and it became second nature for the dogs to remain silent when working. When the leather collar was off, barking was permitted, but after this training our dogs rarely barked unless a stranger entered the kennel area.

Our methods of training were simple and are no doubt familiar to civilians who have owned and trained dogs themselves. The difference was less in spirit than in degree. In the field, something as straightforward as a Sit command could be a life-or-death matter. For this reason it was essential that the handler know his dog as well as the dog knew the commands. Each dog reacted to stimuli in different ways, and each handler had to recognize his dog's particular signals. Some dogs lifted their heads to alert to danger, others sniffed or pointed with their noses in the direction of the noise or scent, and some raised the hackles on their backs when they suspected something ahead.

It would not be long before the men and the dogs were applying what they had learned. A mandatory requirement for all Marines was the camp obstacle course. Every man and dog went through it until they became proficient at completing it. For the dogs it began with open barrels: three barrels, one on top of two, were welded to-gether. The handler left his dog at one end of a barrel and then called him from the other in an attempt to get the dog to come through. Some dogs refused to cooperate, and in desperation, their handlers crawled through the barrel while dragging the dogs through by their leashes. After the dogs learned to crawl through the bottom barrels, they graduated to leaping through the top barrel. The dogs and their handlers practiced this until a whole squad of dogs could advance toward the barrels on a dead run and then fly through whichever barrel the handler designated.

High-jump courses were also constructed. The dogs began by jumping over boards two and a half feet high, and slats were nailed to higher boards until the dogs were hitting the boards at about six feet and scaling the remainder of the wall. Lucky, a black Doberman handled by Pfc. Ed Topka, from Toledo, Ohio, was the champion. At a dead run, Lucky could hit the boards at about seven feet and scratch his way to the summit and over into Topka's waiting arms on the other side of the wall. His record? Nine feet, eight inches.

A-frame structures, eight feet high, were constructed to improve the dog's strength as they scampered up one side and slowly de-scended the other. To improve the dogs' balance, the men fashioned two sets of A-frames, connecting them with a ridgepole. On either end, a railroad tie joined the apex and slanted down to the ground. The dog climbed up one slanting tie, crossed on the narrow ridge-pole and descended on the other slanting tie on the far side. The clumsier dogs lost their balance and fell into the arms of their han-dlers below. Some were so clumsy, in fact, that a handler had to be placed on each side as the dog crossed, until he learned to maneuver on his own. But once they got the hang of it, the dogs could cross a stream on a narrow log and breeze to the other side on a dead run.

As the days passed, new obstacles were added: barbed wire was strung about eighteen inches above the ground and the handlers and their dogs crawled beneath it for twenty yards; machine-gun fire (blanks, of course) above the wire netting encouraged men and dogs to keep their heads down; and trenches fifty feet long and about two feet deep, lined with concrete and filled with water. Wider pools were excavated and the dogs were taught to jump over them. The pools were then excavated and the dogs made to jump over increasingly wide puddles, until a twelve-foot pool could be crossed in a single giant leap. Then the dogs were put in at one end and made to swim the length of the pool by the handler tugging on the leash. All animals swim naturally, so teaching them to swim was not really necessary. But the practice would come in handy when the dogs would wade with the men to the beaches of the islands of the Pacific.

A mock-up of the side of a ship was even constructed between two 15-foot telephone poles planted in the ground 15 feet apart by nailing boards to the poles. A cargo net was slung over the front so that it resembled the side of a ship ready to discharge Marines from the ship to waiting landing craft below, and on the back of the wall the handlers could climb steps to a platform three feet below the top.

For this exercise the dogs wore a special harness made of webbing straps with a ring on top and one at the bottom behind the front legs. A thirty-foot leash was attached to each ring and thrown to a handler below to steady the dog as it was lowered. The dog was then hoisted over the side, and the handler on top would gradually lower the dog to a handler below. Although the dogs never objected to the drill, their paws occasionally got tangled in the net. To avoid this the man at the bottom had to stand ten to fifteen feet from the net and pull the dog away from the net.

The exercise soon became a favorite of visiting VIPs and news reporters, and pictures were taken and published in papers all over the country. Hollywood loved to show the dogs being lowered over the side. Perhaps this was what, in their minds, made Marine dogs different from all other war dogs: they were seagoing.

Both men and dogs confronted basic training with energy and perseverance. The exercises were difficult and the standards strict, but we confronted these hurdles as a team, and celebrated together when they were overcome. Other challenges, too, sorely tried both men and dogs at Camp Lejeune, and man and animal bonded together as they faced them. Mosquitoes, chiggers and scorpions three to four inches long tortured us night and day, with man and beast alike suffering from their sting. No one died as a result, but several dogs were sick enough to require intravenous drips of saline and glucose to fight dehydration. We learned to turn our boots upside down and shake hard before putting them on.

White Oak Swamp emptied into the New River at Jacksonville, North Carolina, and part of it encompassed our camp, irrigating marshy land that made a natural habitat for snakes of all kinds. In addition to several species of nonvenomous vipers, there were rattlesnakes, cottonmouths and copperheads with venom drop-for-drop as poisonous as that of a rattler. Because of the snakebite danger, all hands were forbidden to go into the field without wearing leggings, which, with our pant legs crammed into them, greatly reduced the chance of fangs penetrating the leg. One day I stepped over a log and my foot landed on top of a coiled copperhead. Fortunately, the heel of my boondocker, as our Marine-issue boots were called, slammed down on his head. When I lifted my heel he slithered back under the log.

Peppy was not so lucky. One day as he crossed the creek to the outer training field, a cottonmouth struck him in his upper lip. Butch, the Doberman with the grin, was right behind Peppy, and as his handler Keith Schaible watched in horror, Butch grabbed the snake behind its head and slung it around until it went limp. Despite Schaible's exhortations to "Put that snake down!" Butch continued to fling it around until it was no longer harmful.

Meanwhile, Peppy began to swell from the bite, and I feared that unless something was done the big black Doberman would die before I could get him back to Stewart. I opened my first-aid kit and injected the dog with a syringe of morphine, and as it began to take effect, I carefully made two cuts across the wound and squeezed hard, forcing out as much of the venom as possible. Applying any kind of pressure such as a tourniquet on Peppy's face was impossible. Under my direction, Schaible and Goldblatt took off their jackets and cut two saplings with their K-Bar knives. When the saplings were cut and the limbs were cleaned off, I threaded one through the armhole in one jacket, down to the bottom, into the bottom of the other jacket and out its armhole. By repeating the procedure on the other side and buttoning the jackets in the center, we thus constructed a sling strong enough to carry Peppy.

By now, the morphine had made Peppy drowsy and he lay quietly as the two men carried him up the trail. By the time they reached the sick bay, Peppy's head had swollen to the size of a football. He was having difficulty breathing, his heart pounding so hard we could see it beating against his ribs.

Stewart saw us coming and quickly grabbed a tracheal cannula from the instrument cabinet. He told the men to get Peppy onto the table and hold him on his side. With cotton saturated with alcohol, he scrubbed Peppy's neck, and using a scalpel he carefully cut into Peppy's neck and into the trachea. Air made a hissing sound as it rushed into Peppy's lungs and his chest heaved several times as he settled into normal breathing.

"Will he be all right?" implored Goldblatt of Stewart.

"We'll have to wait and see."

Stewart placed a suction cup over the cut in Peppy's lip and began to withdraw blood, serum, and some of the poison. When the fluid stopped coming, Stewart infiltrated antivenin throughout the area around the bite wound.

For the two days that Peppy's life hung in the balance, Goldblatt refused to leave his side. By the third day the swelling began to subside; by the end of a week it was still the size of a golf ball. Stewart lanced it to release the remaining puss, removed the cannula from Peppy's trachea and covered the wound with a bandage and Vaseline. Recovery was uneventful, and Peppy was back in the field in three weeks.

Basic training was nearing an end, and we were spending more time in the field and less on the training grounds. By now the same men that looked like children when I first saw them now had gained weight and begun to look like Marines. They had gotten over their apprehensions about being assigned to an outfit that they had never dreamed existed. More important, the dogs had become their friends. The look on Goldblatt's face had told me that the ancient bond between animal and man had again been cemented.

★   ★   ★

An unexpected and tragic event caused basic training to come to an early conclusion. Every Thursday morning the dogs and handlers were exposed to the kinds of explosives that would be encountered in combat, though only demolition experts were allowed to actually handle the explosives. Two weeks before the scheduled completion of basic training, a massive demolition exercise was planned for the War Dog Training School, and I joined Gunnery Sergeant Holdren to observe the fireworks. The field looked like a true battlefield: smoke and dust billowed up into the air forming a black artillery cloud that hung over us. The noise was deafening as Dago bombs exploded on the ground and sent more charges flying into the air, where they exploded again. Dogs and their handlers slowly crawled their way across the grass in a prone position while quarter-pound cans of TNT were thrown around them.

Lieutenant Wilson Davis, supervising the operation, was supposed to leave the setting of the explosives in the hands of the demolition experts. But he did not. Carried away by the excitement, he began to set off Dago bombs and accidentally set off an entire box. The resulting explosion caused severe burns and lacerations to his face and arms.

Basic training was scheduled for two more weeks, but Davis would not return for several weeks, maybe more. Captain Boyd turned to me—I was to start advanced field training immediately with the assistance of Gunnery Sergeant Holdren. As an afterthought, Boyd added that he had put in for the officer who was to take command of one of the platoons.

The next day Holdren took me beyond the edges of the camp to show me the preparations he had made for the men. He had designed a course full of all kinds of traps and ambushes similar to those the men could expect to encounter in combat. Trails wandered through brush so thick it was impossible to see for more than two feet beyond either side of the trail, and camouflaged foxholes, slit trenches, bunkers, caves and machine-gun nests lay hidden in that brush. Men in padded suits armed with sacks would occupy the ambushes, and if the dogs got close without discovering an ambush, the men were to jump out and flail threateningly at them. They would not hurt the dogs, of course, but they would scare them enough to make sure that they would never again be caught unaware.

An oak tree that looked like any other from the front had cut into its back a platform wide enough for a man to stand on, and two leather straps made from rifle slings were fastened to the trunk to hold a man securely while he fired a BAR (Browning automatic rifle) through the fork in the tree. Gunny said that if our men and dogs master these obstructions, they would be able to handle almost anything they would find in combat.

I commended him on the thorough job he had done and told him to draw some field telephones and string them along the trail. One man and his dog from each squad would work their way through the course applying the skills they had learned in basic training while the rest of the men in the squad, without their dogs, would act as infantrymen on patrol.

Gunny figured that with twenty-four scout dogs in each platoon we should have them all through in about two weeks. I reminded him that we also had twelve messenger dogs in each platoon and that every Marine has to "do his time in the infantry" whether he would later fly airplanes or carry messages in his collar. He also would have at least one extra Marine to train.

"Who is that, Lieutenant?"

"Me."

★ ★ ★

Gunny Holdren and I were waiting at the trail the next morning when the first three squads arrived. We had chosen Ben Dickerson and his Shepherd Pal to scout the course the first time.

Pfc. Benjamin A. Dickerson III, from Alexandria, Virginia, was just nineteen, slender—almost skinny—with steel gray eyes and straight brown hair. He was more serious than most of the other men: he smiled rarely and walked stealthily—as if ready to strike at any moment. He once said he joined the Marine Corps to kill Japs, but none of us really knew why he had such a hatred for the Japanese. It was rumored that he had a brother on the Bataan Death March. Dickerson neither confirmed nor denied it.

Pal, a gray German Shepherd with a black saddle extending from his shoulders to the base of his tail, was enlisted in the Corps when his owner, a Marine sergeant at Montford Point, received orders for overseas duty. Unable to take Pal with him, the owner had walked Pal over the bridge to our camp and signed him up for the duration of the war. Pal was almost as tough as Dickerson, and responded instantly to his handler's commands, yelping and slashing with his fangs. But when Ben gave the command Out, the storm subsided, and Pal calmed down as if nothing had ever happened.

Dickerson and Pal would take the "point"—the first position in the column of men, from five up to fifty yards in front, depending on visibility—with another young sergeant named Billy Baldwin. Another man, Pfc. Edward Topka, a stocky eighteen-year-old with a round ruddy face and a hint of an East European accent, was picked as the infantry scout to follow between Dickerson and Baldwin, while the rest of the squad acted as the patrol. (Normally, Topka handled Lucky; today Lucky—and all the other dogs—would stay back in camp.) Ambushes and simulated enemy machine-gun positions lay ahead, and it would be Pal's job to find them and the squad's job to eliminate them.

Pal would work off-leash in front of Dickerson. If he alerted, Dickerson was to give him the Down signal and immediately notify the patrol leader, Sergeant Baldwin. The system would be the same as any normal rifle company patrol—only the dog was unusual.

The logic of the patrol was simple. Traditionally, the point man, or scout, would encounter the enemy first and warn the squad. But in the thick jungles of Guadalcanal, the Japanese had often let the scout pass, then attacked the rest of the column from their hidden position. We theorized that the Japanese could hide from a scout but never from his dog.

Baldwin gave his squad orders for the first practice run: not to bunch up, to keep five paces between each other, and if the handler held up his arm, the men were to stop and take cover at the sides of the trail.

Dickerson removed Pal's chain collar and replaced it with the leather one. He made a throwing motion and Pal bounded down the trail looking for the expected object. He searched the sides of the trail without success and turned back toward Dickerson who again made the throwing motion. Pal understood and proceeded, looking back at his master every few steps for continued cues. The patrol fanned out behind Dickerson, with Topka five yards behind Dickerson, followed by Baldwin, followed by the rest of the men. Gunny and I walked behind Baldwin so that we could observe.

Fifty yards down the trail, Pal alerted and stopped. He perked his ears straight up and began to show interest in something ahead. He reminded me of a dog running down a country path that suddenly catches sight or scent of some unseen bird and stops cold. Dickerson made a slow whistle through his teeth. It was inaudible more than a few feet away, but Pal heard it. He turned and looked at his master, who raised his arm. Pal froze. Dickerson's arm came slowly down in a sweeping arc, and Pal immediately dropped to the ground. Dickerson held his arm out in front of his body, his wrist bent backward so that the heel of his hand faced Pal, and moved his palm toward Pal in a jerking motion, a signal for Pal to stay, then turned to Topka and told him that there was something ahead.

Baldwin, who saw Pal freeze, motioned the squad to take cover and told Gunny Holdren. Gunny explained the situation to me: on the right side of the trail ahead, two men were stationed in a foxhole, a favorite trick of the Japanese. Throughout the islands of the Pacific, they dug foxholes behind the bushes on either side of a trail, and if a patrol came in sight, they would wait until it was within throwing distance before cutting loose with a shower of hand grenades. If the men on patrol bunched up, one grenade would kill several of them. "Stay away from each other," he said, "you'll live longer."

Gunny lowered his voice and spoke slowly and deliberately. He told the men that they were going to have to learn these lessons well or they, not the dog, would be the warning device. Then he explained that to remove an ambush of this kind, the patrol should fire at it, keeping the occupants pinned down until one of the men could crawl forward and destroy the position with hand grenades.

The patrol was allowed to pass on through the ambush, and Pal was sent out again. Although he showed some signs of tension, a possible indication of danger up ahead, the Shepherd did not alert. Suddenly, a practice grenade flew into the air followed closely by another. The grenades exploded harmlessly on the far side as a man holding a burlap sack burst out of the brush and began flailing at Pal.

Dickerson ordered Pal to attack, and the dog leaped forward, snarling fiercely and grabbing his tormentor's arm. He missed and was slapped in the face and on the front legs with the sack, but lunged again and grabbed the sack in his teeth. The agitator slung Pal around, kicking him. Padded shin pads battered Pal's stomach. The dog released the sack and charged the man's chest, knocking him down. He jumped on the fallen man and slashed at his arms and throat. "Out, Pal, Out," commanded Dickerson. Immediately, Pal backed off and stood ready to charge again if the man so much as twitched. Dickerson praised Pal and patted him on the shoulder. On command, Pal turned and heeled alongside Dickerson's left knee.

When we got to the curve in the trail, Gunny stopped the men and instructed them to always let their patrol leader know when there was a curve ahead so he would have time to deploy his men. They were then to sneak around the curve using bushes as cover, or crawl to stay concealed. When the trail ahead could be seen, they were to send the dog out and watch him very closely. If the dog alerted to anything down the straightaway, he was to be recalled immediately: it might prevent the dog's being killed. These dogs were not expendable—they could be replaced only from the States.

Other exercises were conducted and other potential ambushes confronted, like BAR men, and snipers. Gunny Holdren warned the men about trees, the favorite places of snipers. Look up into the trees, look down at the ground, look into the brush, look everywhere, he said. Death usually comes from wherever it is least expected. The men would have to make up their minds: it would be them or the Japanese.

Dickerson and Pal were by now a well-oiled team, ready to take on anything. Pal was sent to the far side of the grove where Dickerson could see and control him. Now and then, air could be heard escaping from between the handler's teeth. At the direction of this soft whistle, Pal worked the trail to the left, then the right, as though pulled from side to side by an invisible string. When Pal was about a hundred yards from the far side of a large meadow, he froze. Dickerson blew through his teeth and Pal bounded back to his side. Dickerson reported to Baldwin that Pal had alerted about fifteen yards to the left of where the trail entered the brush. Baldwin scanned the area with his field glasses, then grinned. Gunny Holdren had cleared a little too much brush, and it was clear where Holdren's men were hidden. Baldwin was right; Gunny had the machine-gun crews stand up.

On islands like Iwo Jima, the Japanese would win respect for their intricate, treacherous networks of caves and refusal to surrender as long as they were left with a hole to crawl into. Flamethrowers would help ferret out hidden Japanese, but unless our men knew which caves to attack, all the flamethrowers in the world would be useless. Gunny had dug caves similar to those that pockmarked Guadalcanal, and as part of the training exercise some of the caves would be occupied, and others would not. If the dogs could tell the difference between the two, they could make a tremendous contribution to the dangerous clean-up efforts on these islands. There the caves had proved so hard to deal with that they were usually just brought under fire to keep them quiet until our Marines were safely past. Then somebody had the job of destroying them, one by one. But even after they were cleared out, stragglers would find them and hole up until they were blown shut or until the Seabees bulldozed the entrances. The caves, he warned, would be full of supplies and good souvenirs, but "stay out of them if you want to live a long and happy life!"

We began this exercise by having Dickerson throw a stick into the entrance of the first cave. Pal rushed after it and immediately reappeared with the wood in his mouth. Dickerson tossed the stick into a second cave. This time, however, an agitator waving his sack met Pal. The dog was so taken by surprise that he lost his balance and fell backward. Quickly scrambling to his feet in a rage, Pal charged his tormentor, and grabbed with a vengeance the sack that beat at him, holding on as he was flung around in the air. The agitator tripped and fell into the creek, and Pal jumped in after him, harassing the struggling man until he screamed for someone to "get the monster off" of him before he drowned.

After that encounter, Pal approached the next cave cautiously. He stretched his neck forward and pointed his nose directly toward the opening. Deciding it was unoccupied, he entered and retrieved the stick. One more cave was found to contain an agitator. This time, as Pal approached, he stopped and raised the hackles on his back and neck.

We worked the trail until every dog had been through the course at least five times. The dogs learned to work on arm and hand signals as well as voice commands; the men learned how patrols were conducted and became expert scouts. Gunny Holdren set up ambushes and defensive positions in other parts of the woods and in fields, and the men and dogs went on patrol after patrol. They learned to be on the alert for enemy lurking everywhere, and they came to believe in and trust their dogs. When the leather collar was placed around their necks, the dogs were eager to work and never missed alerting to someone ahead.

Then the roles were reversed. The dogs were stationed in prepared positions and an attempt was made to approach undetected. It was gratifying to see that the dogs knew instinctively what was wanted of them: nobody could come near without the dogs warning their handlers of an intrusion. The messenger dogs were just as good at this as the scout dogs, so I felt it would be advantageous to have them equally well trained.

Night problems—always difficult for ordinary Marines—were a cinch: the dogs could alert when humans were as far away as several hundred yards, a feat that amazed Gunny Holdren. He was delighted that the dogs wouldn't bark, and tickled that we would know when the Japanese were coming but they would not know we were lying in wait for them. "And that, Lieutenant," he liked to say, "puts you in the driver's seat." There was no doubt now that these Marines with dogs were going to be an asset in combat.

Some of the dogs, however, were not sharp enough to complete the course satisfactorily. I asked to have these dogs replaced, but my request was denied. We would have to take them through our first invasion before we were allowed to replace them. We used them to guard foxholes at night, but we never allowed them to lead patrols. The danger was too great for the dogs, their handlers and the Marines they were leading: incompetent scouting was a deadly formula.

Gunny Holdren was full of good advice based on his experiences. He expounded on how best to conduct patrols and offered a few more suggestions: he recommended that I keep the men busy. They were all pretty young and full of themselves. That was good for combat, when energy was needed and usually in short supply, but with little to do and too much time, they could give me a lot of trouble. If they couldn't find anybody else to fight, they'd fight among themselves.

As usual, the Gunny was right. The men had gained a lot of weight and a lot of confidence. I thought to myself that these boys would have to fight to gain their place in the Corps because an outfit as different as a war dog unit is bound to be made fun of—barked at, even.

★　★　★

Lieutenant Stanley Perigoe Hayter came from Hollywood, California. A movie producer before and after the war, he was recruited to train mine detection dogs. Some of the Japanese mines were made of clay or ceramics, and although they exploded with the same destructive power as metal mines, the magnetic mine detectors were incapable of locating them. These ceramic mines were covered with khaki and resembled a surveyor's tape, leading us to call them "tape measure" mines. They could easily blow a man's legs off.

After the dogs were trained, they could be relied upon to discover all mines—antitank, antipersonnel, metallic or nonmetallic—as well as trip wires, booby traps and almost any buried objects, day or night. The dogs indicated the exact location of these objects by stopping one to three paces in front of the actual location of the object, then sitting and refusing to move forward.

Unfortunately, in fields that had been shelled by artillery, the dogs alerted to shrapnel in the ground, which made their use under this circumstance worthless. In later years, we overcame this problem by training dogs to be more selective. The green-jacketed Beagles of the Agriculture Department used at airports, for example, are trained to be sensitive to food products; narcotic-detecting dogs are trained to sniff out exclusively narcotics, other dogs to spot just explosives.

The men selected to train mine detection dogs were first sent to an engineering school, where they completed a course in mine detection. I sat in on their lectures to better learn about how the enemy placed mines. Some lessons were in human nature: all men act in a similar way when striving for similar goals under like conditions whether they are Japanese or American. We Americans buried mines the same way—and in the same places—as the Japanese. When we approached an area where we would have planted mines, we learned to be aware that the Japanese might have planted mines there as well.

The dogs trained in mine detection by the Marine Corps in World War II were all Doberman Pinschers. To be a good mine detection dog, the dog must be absolutely sound, emotionally stable and have an exceptionally good nose. It was imperative that the handler study his dog's behavior in all circumstances, working, feeding, grooming and even playing.

The mine detection dog and his handler began and ended basic training together. The training, like the training for patrol dogs, was one of repetition and progression. First a small steel trap was placed on the ground in plain sight. The handler walked the dog toward the object and placed his paw in the trap. The blades of the trap were padded with rubber and produced only a pinching sensation, but the surprise of the trap snapping on his foot was of great concern to the dog. He howled, cried, or whined not because the trap hurt him but because he was surprised. He tried to relieve himself of the trap by shaking his foot or biting the trap, which was seldom successful.

The handler waited for a few seconds and hurriedly removed the trap and threw it away. At the same time, he expressed fear and horror of the trap. He tried to impress upon the dog that the trap was something that the dog should also react to with horror and always be on the alert for. When the trap had been thrown away, the handler hugged the dog, petted him, praised him and assured him that together the two of them would be safe. This procedure was repeated until the dog learned to look for the trap. When he found it, he was praised and the trap was danced around as if being cursed and then hurled into the brush.

After the dogs became proficient at finding the traps in plain sight, they were covered with grass or leaves and the dog was made to put his foot in the hidden trap. The dog then began to use his nose to find it. When he found it, he was again praised, petted and encouraged to continue his efforts at finding traps.

Once the dog learned to find the traps under grass and leaves, the traps were buried. Our dogs could find even objects that had been buried for long periods of time. In one instance, the engineers had constructed a minefield for use in their own exercises, and then plowed it with bulldozers. When we saw the course, it had been raining on it once or twice a week for six months. The dogs were still able to find 96 percent of the mines. When a mine was discovered, the dog sat and the location was staked. The dog was then walked around the spot and continued quartering the field until the entire area was covered.

The training on trip wires made use of the electrical shock from the coil in a cattle-fence mechanism. The dog received a shock when he touched the wire, and, as with the traps, he gradually began to watch for it and then to use his nose to find it. Trip wires were used extensively in the Pacific Theater across trails and in openings to caves and doorways to abandoned buildings, the wires attached to explosives that were set to explode when tripped. The dogs' sense of hearing was so acute that they could hear the wire singing from even a slight breeze.

Booby traps of all kinds were wired to explode when moved. Souvenirs were likely to be trapped, and sometimes the Japanese even trapped their own dead. Some of our scout dogs were trained (surreptitiously) by their handlers to find trip wires and booby traps by continually encouraging them to search until the dogs were on the alert for anything unusual in front of them. The handlers recognized the ability of the dogs to accomplish this and felt that this would prevent both the dog and the handler from stumbling into trip wires, antipersonnel mines or booby-trapped material found in caves. They used the same technique of affectionate reward used in other training, and it worked; our dogs never got caught.

It was fascinating to watch the dogs being trained for this work, and to this day I am not sure how dogs are able to find things that have been buried for long periods of time. All dogs, of course, bury their bones and belongings and leave them, buried, sometimes for a period of years. In spite of rain, snow and frozen earth, when the dog wants his bone, he just digs it up. Has the dog remembered where his treasure was buried? He has not; his nose has shown him the way.

Unlike the work done with our scout dogs on the sly, the official Marine Corps method of training mine detection dogs was the "fear method." Fear is a powerful emotion, self-preservation the most powerful of all human and animal instincts. In this case, the fear was perfectly rational: if a mistake were to be made in detecting a mine, the handler and the dog would be killed or mutilated, depending on the power of the mine's explosive. But the method was not a sound one. During the early training, the dog may become spooked by all metallic things—including his feed pan—and refuse to eat. Some dogs would shake in fear at the sight of their food pans. The handlers had to overcome this by feeding the dog by hand, gradually moving his hand closer to the pan over a period of days and finally dropping the food into the pan while he reassured the dog that it was safe to eat.

The fear instilled by this training was so overwhelming, in fact, that the dogs could only be worked for short periods of time. After forty-five minutes or so, the dogs would shake with stress. They began to make mistakes, and if pressed too far, they would sit and refuse to work at all. So then we worked them for only thirty minutes at a time, leaving them the other thirty of every hour for rest and play.

But some dogs were not capable of being trained. A few of the ones that could not take the training seemed never to fully recover from their experiences. Even after attempts to detrain them, they remained jumpy and would spook at the slightest stimulus. The dogs trained unofficially, on the other hand, did not experience any stress because they were taught to do something that seemed both natural and fun. The handlers had never heard about the fear method and just used common sense. Today the fear method is no longer used.

I have watched today's dogs working at airports and border crossings. They enjoy it and give no indication to me that they are in mortal fear while doing it. They wag their tails and search as if they were playing a game to be relished. The sign on the little Department of Agriculture Beagles says OUR DOGS DON'T BITE. The look on their faces, as they sit in front of you and peer into your eyes, says "Gotcha." Are they motivated by fear? I think not. They are playing a game that they always win.

Training of mine detection dogs in the Marine Corps in World War II was not our finest hour. In spite of the fact that the dogs were fantastic in their ability to detect all kinds of objects, the emotional cost to the dogs was severe, the damage bordering on the inhumane despite the worthiness of the cause. Only six mine detection dogs were ever sent to combat. All of them survived the war and were returned to civilian life.

★　★　★

The final task for which dogs were used was the carrying of messages and light, precious supplies. Whenever a Marine runner is called for, a messenger dog can be used instead. The dog presents a smaller target, has greater speed and can traverse difficult terrain much easier and faster than a man.

The training begins with the two handlers standing several feet apart. The messenger collar (a canvas collar with a zippered pocket for the message) is placed on the dog and the handler points to his partner and commands, "Report, Report." As soon as the command Report is given, the second handler calls and the dog responds by going to him. This procedure is continued and the distance between the handlers is gradually increased until they are several hundred yards apart. At this point, the handler that is to receive the message hides. If the dog has difficulty finding the handler, the handler calls the dog, which completes the exercise.

This is repeated until the dog begins to use his nose to follow the trail of his callers. When the dog advances sufficiently in training to find the handlers in fixed positions, the handlers begin to move. The dog now has to track the handlers to find them. This is necessary because in combat the command post is constantly being moved as the battle progresses and the dog must be able to track his handlers wherever they go. When the dog can be depended upon to report to his other handler regardless of his position, distractions, or weather, day and night, the training is complete.

Our best messenger dog was Missy, a white German Shepherd that came to us in the original shipment of dogs we got from the Army. She was a beautiful dog and one of the many successful females that we had. We did not specify that our dogs be male or female, spayed or neutered, and we were not allowed to alter them because they were to be returned intact to their original owners at the end of the war. When the females were in heat, they were not worked with the males, but nonetheless, as one might expect, we had puppies from time to time.

Missy was assigned to Pfc.'s Claude Sexton and Earl Wright. She could run faster than any Shepherd I ever saw, and she would do anything to get from one of them to the other: swim rivers under fire, traverse fields with explosions, and crash through jungle vines and brush. Pathé News filmed Missy carrying messages and ammunition and showed the clip, to great acclaim, in theaters all over the country. This propensity to run from one handler to the other, in spite of all odds, ended later in tragedy in the jungles of Guam.

The 2nd and 3rd War Dog Platoons did not use messenger dogs to any extent in combat. By the time we arrived in the Pacific, communication equipment was so improved and dependable that dogs were no longer useful for carrying messages. Tubby carried one or two messages between his handlers, Pfc.'s Mason Wachstetter and Vincent Salvaggio, which was about the extent of our use of messenger dogs.

The primary value of our dogs lay in scouting, in exploring caves and pillboxes, or as sentries. We eventually turned our messenger dogs into scout dogs, and they performed admirably. After the Guam campaign the commanding general of the 3rd Marine Division, General Alfred Noble, recommended that war dog platoons utilize only scout dogs, and called for fifty-four scout dogs instead of twenty-four scout dogs and twelve messenger dogs. Alas, this recommendation was not followed and the Corps continued to train unusable messenger dogs until the end of the war.

The thought of the dogs crashing through the jungle or crawling wounded the last few feet in mud and rain to save a position of Marines surrounded by enemy troops was just too much to give up, it seemed. Every schoolchild of my generation read about the valiant efforts of Cher Ami, the carrier pigeon of World War I, flying through shellfire and dodging German sharpshooters. She arrived at her loft with a broken wing and a message attached to her leg from a French battalion that was surrounded by Germans. By her valiant efforts, the battalion was saved. Cher Ami survived to become a French national hero.

★ ★ ★

Midway through the summer, Second Lieutenant William T. Taylor, a graduate of Louisiana State University, arrived to take over one of the two newly formed war dog platoons. He had been stationed at the Rifle Range when the call went out for a line officer to serve with the war dogs. Certain that the Rifle Range was a dead end, he applied for the job and was accepted.

Taylor was a tall, wiry twenty-five-year-old with dark hair and deep-set eyes. He had attended college on a baseball scholarship and moved with the agility and speed of an athlete. He was a naturally friendly person who was equally comfortable being serious when the occasion called for it—and he was a natural leader. He arrived with his sea bag over his shoulder and approached me with a big smile and his free hand extended. He said he had been sent over here to take over a war dog platoon, whatever that was.

I laughed and filled him in on the training sequence. Captain Boyd, too, told Taylor he was glad to have him aboard. Getting down to business, he said that Taylor got his commission on February 4 and I got mine on February 9. Taylor, therefore, would get the 2nd Platoon and I would take the 3rd. Taylor was new, so Boyd assigned Sergeant Raymond Barnowsky to the 2nd Platoon and Sergeant Ivan Hamilton, who was new, to my 3rd.

So began a relationship that existed for the entire time the two platoons were together. Taylor and I never let disagreements interfere with our duties, and what few disagreements we had were settled quietly and amiably. We always worked as a duo and made together the decisions that were the best for the platoons. It was one of the most satisfactory relationships that I have ever had, and our compatibility saved the lives of many of our men and dogs.

Once the platoons were divided, we began to work with one on defense and the other on attack. We continued this for the remainder of the time we were to stay at Camp Lejeune, drilling in the field constantly. Patrolling was repeated and repeated until it became second nature, and night maneuvers conducted in which one platoon would try to infiltrate the other and vice versa, sparring in this manner until midnight or one o'clock in the morning. The men and dogs soon became so adept at defense that the infiltrating team served only as a training mechanism for the defending team—the infiltrators always got caught. By summer's end, we knew that in combat nobody could sneak into our position undetected. Gunny was the happiest of all: "I sure would have liked to have had them dogs on the Canal." By those who had been there, Guadalcanal was always reffered to as "the Canal."

We also went on long hikes, some as long as twenty-five miles, and the men and dogs took them in stride. The platoons were ready. November came and we got our orders to ship out on November 5. One thing troubled me. Captain Boyd, otherwise fairly competent, had refused to provide me with an adequately equipped sick bay for the dogs. The only medical supplies we carried with us were in our first-aid kits. Even Jim Stewart attempted to intervene, but Boyd held firm. The upshot was that once we left Camp Lejeune we had no medical supplies for treating the dogs if they became sick or injured.

★　★　★

A parade was scheduled for our final day at Camp Lejeune. The Montford Point Band was there to send off the 2nd and 3rd War Dog Platoons, a real treat because the Montford Point Band was the finest on base. The Special Services officer for Montford Point was Captain Bobby Troup, the composer of the songs "Daddy" and "Route 66." He took great pride in his band and rightly so, and we were all very pleased and excited to host him.

My mother, father and brother came down from Virginia to watch the parade and say goodbye. My brother Julian brought his little dog, Bobby, and enlisted him into the 2nd and 3rd War Dog Platoons as our mascot. Bobby was the size of a Cocker Spaniel with the body of a Dachshund. On first sight he looked amazingly like a B-17. His large ears stuck out from his head at right angles and he had a congenital short tail. I turned Bobby over to Sergeant Hamilton, and he became everybody's pet, sleeping in whatever tent suited him that night. He was the only dog that didn't know anything. The men refused to train him at all; they said Bobby should remain "free." So Bobby trained them: they did exactly what he wanted.

CHAPTER THREE

CAMP PENDLETON, CALIFORNIA

The train that took us to Camp Pendleton consisted of three Pull-man sleepers, five baggage cars, one diner and one caboose. It was exclusively for the transport of the 2nd and 3rd War Dog Platoons. The dogs were loaded into the baggage cars in their crates and the train left the siding at 6 P.M. While the dogs rode in the back, Bill Taylor and I each had our own compartment, which were first class compared to the double-deckers assigned to the men. But nobody complained—we were beginning our great adventure.

The first night out we had turkey, giblet gravy and mashed pota-toes even though Thanksgiving was still three weeks away. It tasted better than anything our mess sergeant at Camp Lejeune had ever served. But there is a price to pay for everything. By midnight the entire complement had food poisoning and a long line of shivering men painfully waited their turn outside the head.

At a stop in Anniston, Alabama, I obtained the paregoric needed, and the men lined up as Sergeant Hamilton poured a spoonful of the wretched, licorice-tasting medicine down each man's throat. By lunchtime the crisis was over, and before dinner the men, in true Marine fashion, were fighting for a place in the chow line.

Frequently, the train pulled over on a siding to let pass a troop train or trains carrying tanks, artillery and other mechanized equipment. Our train must have had the lowest priority in the entire United States military because we sat on sidings for several hours every day. For the men it was an opportunity to get the dogs out of their crates and exercise them in adjacent wooded areas and valleys, on hillsides, or sometimes just up and down the tracks.

When we were moving and could not get the dogs outside to relieve themselves, the men brought them to a particular baggage car where we had spread wood shavings two or three inches deep on the floor. The men swept up the shavings and waste daily, and the barrels were emptied when we stopped in the countryside. Once a day we washed the floor with interior hoses and put down new shavings to start the process all over again.

As an added incentive for the dogs, the police sergeant at Lejeune had built and presented as a going-away present four large wooden fire hydrants painted bright red. Unfortunately, the sergeant did not use adequate paint, because the red soon shriveled and peeled under the assault of the dogs. They did not mind, however, and continued to spray them down as if they were the real things.

At feeding time, the men stood in line with their dogs' pans, and a mixture of dry meal, or kibble, mixed with canned dog food was ladled into each. The dogs were then taken from their crates and fed in the clear area in the center of the car. Only twelve dogs could eat at one time in each car, so it took several shifts to get them all fed. Feeding the dogs in their crates was forbidden because some of the dogs had a bad habit of spilling their food or turning over their feed pans, and although we had hoses in the cars to wash out the cages or wash the dogs, if needed, it was done only when necessary.

We saw our first cowboy in Arkansas and our first snow in New Mexico. When the train stopped, as usual, to let others go by, Taylor and I decided to let the men and dogs off to exercise. On the right side of the train, a hillside rose gradually for a mile before it reached a wooded area. Released from their crates, the dogs raced up the snow-covered slope, the German Shepherds plowing through the snow leaving a deep furrow, and the Dobermans leaping above it in giant graceful bounds. For the seventy-two dogs it was a wonderful respite from their confining life aboard the lurching train and the previous months of hard training.

The men, too, welcomed the break. Some of them wrestled with their dogs in the new snow, and a few snowball fights broke out as well. When the train whistle sounded, the two- and four-legged creatures all rushed down the hill, tripping each other and rolling in the snow to make the fun last as long as possible. The sun was setting as a tired and happy bunch climbed aboard the train and we headed west again.

Late one afternoon the train stopped for an hour in the middle of Gallup, New Mexico, where, along the tracks, local Mexican and Indian women had set up large pots of hot food. As the men stepped off the train, the women thrust paper plates filled with food into our hands. Most of us were from the East, and had never before eaten tamales, tacos, refried beans, rice and enchiladas. They were delicious, and as soon as we finished one plate, the women shoved another at us.

I was delighted, but puzzled by their generosity, and our train's conductor, seeing the confusion on my face, explained that the women fed all the troop trains heading west that stopped at the station. The entire New Mexico National Guard had been in the Philippines and were captured when Bataan fell to the Japanese, he explained. Most were of Mexican or Indian heritage. When they were captured, nearly every family lost someone. "They hope that if enough Marines head west and on to the Pacific, someday their men will come home," he said.

As we pulled out of the station, the women stood by their pots with a forlorn look on their faces and their arms hanging loosely at their sides, watching us until we were out of sight. Only when the Japanese were defeated in 1945, and after spending more than three and a half years in prisoner of war camps, did their men come home.

★ ★ ★

I had just gotten to my compartment one night when Hamilton summoned me to the baggage car. Spike, it seemed, had injured his back leg jumping back into the baggage car after we exercised the dogs before heading west again. The train had lurched just as Spike jumped into the door and it threw him off balance, knocking him against a large nail that protruded about two inches from the bottom of the door jam. I hurried through the swaying cars as the train snaked its way through the hills. When I entered the car, blood was everywhere. Pfc. Bob Johnson, one of Spike's handlers, was struggling to hold the messenger dog down while putting pressure on the spot from which blood was spurting. "He's going to bleed to death if you don't do something, Lieutenant," Johnson cried.

"Take it easy," I said.

When Johnson let go of Spike's leg, blood shot halfway up the wall. I kneeled and grabbed the leg. The blood was coming from the inner side of the thigh, about midway between the knee and his groin. I squeezed hard above the puncture and pushed my thumb deep into the femoral furrow, the trough dividing the muscles covering the arteries and nerves leading to the lower leg. The bleeding stopped.

I asked Hamilton to break out three or four rolls of bandage from the first-aid kits stored in a nearby cardboard box. The kits, which opened like sardine cans, were made of metal with hooks that attached to a Marine's cartridge belt, and every Marine carried one. They contained bandages, a Syrette of morphine, sulfa pills and iodine. Those in the box were spares.

Ivan thrust a roll of gauze at me, and I placed it into the furrow just above the wound, pressed hard and told Hamilton to start wrapping bandages around his leg and my hand as tightly as he could. He rolled one and then another around Spike's leg. I removed my hand and waited to see if the hemorrhage was under control. There was no sign of blood seeping through. I added two more rolls of bandage and secured the last one by splitting the ends and tying them. I gave Spike a pat on the head and told Johnson to keep him quiet.

Tomaszewski was standing by and I told him to give Spike two sulfa pills every four hours and to keep watch over him. If blood seeped through the bandage, or if his leg began to swell, he was to come and get me on the double. I didn't want the circulation to be cut off—it could cause gangrene. I would be back later, and if everything was proceeding without problems, would change Spike's bandage.

"It's a good thing you're a vet, Lieutenant," said Ski, "or Spike would have bled to death."

I was glad, too. I just wished that I had a fully equipped sick bay for the dogs.

★ ★ ★

It was dark when we crossed the California border at Needles. The conductor said we would arrive at Camp Pendleton early in the morning. The train stopped several times during the night to change engines and direction: to get to Camp Pendleton, the train was switched to tracks that went south from San Bernardino toward San Diego. The last change took place about 2 A.M. I went to sleep in my bunk, and when I awoke, it was beginning to get light.

The train jolted to a stop, and I raised the shade on the window and looked out on a small wooden railroad station. A sign at the end of the building spelled out in large capital letters SAN ONOFRE, CALIFORNIA. Beyond the stationhouse was a wide beach on which the surf of the Pacific Ocean roared as it crashed upon the shore.

Across the road stood an old stucco building with a neon sign that read SAN ONOFRE CAFÉ. Two hand-operated gasoline pumps stood in the gravel driveway, and small lights announced ON PREMISES, WINE AND BEER and gave the store's alcohol license number. We were in California, but little had changed. If the store had been picked up and set down on U.S. Highway 29 outside Opelika, Alabama, nothing would have been different except the ABC permit number and the Pacific Ocean across the way. San Onofre, California, consisted of one small train station, one honky-tonk, no houses, no factories, no stores and no people. (With the addition of a nuclear electric generating plant and the absence of the San Onofre Café, it remains just as exciting today.)

Just then someone called out to me. I looked up and saw a fat lieutenant coming toward me with a big grin on his face. It was Bob Dowell, a 240-pound football star from the University of Texas and a classmate at Quantico. He said that when he found out he was meeting a contingent of dogs, he figured I might be with them. He grabbed me by the hand and gave it a vigorous shake. "Welcome to California."

★　★　★

We arrived at Tent Camp 2, Camp Pendleton, the same day our train pulled in to San Onofre, and found our tents were already set up—two hundred yards beyond the rest of the camp. A large open area was available to kennel the dogs, and I told the men to arrange the crates, which would serve as doghouses from now on, in rows at least forty feet apart. That would leave plenty of room between each dog. We drove in steel stakes with twelve-foot chains and tethered the dogs to them. The stakes had swivel snaps on the top so the dogs wouldn't get tangled up in the chain as they moved about. We had two large tents; we used one to store supplies, the other to store and prepare the dog food. By the end of the day, all the dogs were properly tethered, the men assigned tents, and Taylor and I had moved into our tent on officers' row behind the fire barn.

At lunch the next day, we met John Antonelli, the commanding officer of the Raider Battalion, which would be sharing Camp Pendleton with us. He was young for a major, but his chest was covered with ribbons. Antonelli was a graduate of the United States Naval Academy at Annapolis, of medium build with dark hair and eyes. He acknowledged us only with a subtle nod of his head. I was not sure he approved of dogs in his battalion.

Later that afternoon an officer in his sixties arrived, introduced himself as Lieutenant Colonel Parsons and asked genially how we had fared on our cross-country trip. We were to report to him on all matters concerning the war dog platoons, and if we had any questions or needs, we were not to hesitate to call on him. I learned from Hamilton that the colonel was known throughout the Corps as "Bug Eyes" because his thick lenses made his eyes appear large and bulging. Parsons also had a reputation for being a holy terror when aggravated.

But I found him helpful when I called on him, as directed, a few days later. Spike was not recovering from the injury he had received on the train. I cleaned the wound several times a day with soap and water and dusted it with powdered sulfanilamide, a new antibacterial medicine in which all wounds were now dusted. Sulfanilamide saved thousands of lives in World War II, but this wound failed to respond. In fact, it had gotten worse, and Spike was now running a fever of 104 degrees.

I told Colonel Parsons that without proper treatment Spike would develop blood poisoning and die. Then I told him that I had no drugs or instruments to properly treat the dogs, and he blew his top.

Never since have I encountered one human being who was more altered by his emotions. His face became distorted and from his collar a wave of crimson rose until it crawled beneath his hat, making his head look like a giant beet. "Are you telling me that they sent you out with these dogs and didn't give you any medical supplies?" he screamed. "I read your record and it clearly stated that you were a licensed veterinarian. Don't you want equipment to take care of your dogs?"

I explained—calmly—that I had asked for a fully equipped sick bay but my request had been turned down. Of course I wanted to take care of the dogs in addition to my other duties, but I had nothing to work with.

Parsons fumed: the dogs had cost the government a lot of money to train and would cost the government more if they died because brass had insisted that I stick to infantry duties. It was a waste of talent, he said, at a time when the Corps needed all the talent and training it could get. Finally, he calmed down and told me to take Spike to a vet named Boyce in the nearby town of Oceanside and have him do whatever was necessary and bill the Corps. In the meantime, he would wire the Bureau of Medicine and Surgery in Washington to authorize me to draw any supplies I needed from Navy medical supply depots.

Hamilton brought the reconnaissance car—a pickuplike vehicle, referred to as a recon, that had an open cab—that had been issued to us, and with Ski and Spike we headed south on U.S. 101 toward Oceanside. In the slow truck, it took an hour to cover the thirty-five miles.

In Oceanside we found the doctor, a small, wizened man wearing a large, wide-brimmed cowboy hat. His head was so small and his hat so big that he had to bend his whole head backward to see forward through the steel-rimmed glasses perched on the end of his nose. To me he looked like a life-sized model for Barney Google, a cartoon character popular at the time.

I told him we had seventy-two dogs at Pendleton and a very sick one outside in the truck. I explained that I was a veterinarian as well as a line officer, but that I had no drugs or equipment for treating the dogs. "If your dogs get sick and you're unable to help them, they won't need you for any line duties," observed Dr. Boyce. He added that we were lucky to have Colonel Parsons on our side; he was crazy about dogs, owned three or four himself and brought them to Dr. Boyce whenever they needed care. As far as cost, he told us not to worry about it and to feel free to use any drugs or equipment that he had available.

Then it was down to business. While Ski laid Spike on the exam table, I gave him the history of Spike's injury and infection and told Boyce the Doberman's temperature was up to 104.5 degrees. The wound would have to be opened to release the fluid and to explore further to find the source of the trouble, and Spike would have to be sedated before we could do this. I asked for a syringe and some Nembutal. Ski already was holding Spike's forearm to cause his vein to stand out, but warned that Spike's blood pressure was low.

Boyce noticed that the injured leg was swollen to twice the size of Spike's other leg and that Spike showed little response to what was happening around him. Spike's temperature was now 105 degrees— it looked like we didn't get him to Boyce any too soon. Boyce began to lay out his instruments in a tray.

I squeezed Spike's foot with a rhythmic motion, pumping blood up the leg. When the vein swelled into sight, I inserted the needle and injected 6cc of Nembutal. Spike relaxed. Pinching the webbing between his toes, there was no response; Spike was completely under.

"He really must be toxic," said Boyce, watching intently. "He took only about half the dose usually required for a dog his size."

I examined the leg until I found a spot so soft that it felt like a tightly inflated balloon. There I inserted a scalpel into the skin and pushed downward; a stream of foul-smelling, yellowish-green pus gushed forth. I enlarged the opening to about three inches; the pus flowed like it was coming from a well. I applied pressure to the leg and expelled the last of the fluid from the wound, then flushed it with an antiseptic to drive out the remnants of corruption.

Boyce handed me a probe twelve inches long that I inserted six inches into the leg. "I can feel the bone," I said, moving the probe gently up and down. "There's a rough spot here. Maybe you had better feel it."

Dr. Boyce's deft fingers guided the probe into the wounded leg. His Barney Google face moved up and down following the probe as if he could see the tip of it through the dog's flesh. Years of practice had given him fingers more discerning than many men's eyes.

He stopped the probe and said the problem was that the periosteum—the tough, fibrous membrane surrounding the bone—had been injured when Spike's leg was punctured and the dog had developed a bone ulcer that would not heal if left alone. Boyce moved a piece of silver nitrate stick about a quarter of an inch long and one-eighth inch in diameter into the wound to cauterize the ulcer and to get rid of the old scar tissue, guiding it up the leg with the probe and gently depositing it on the roughened bone.

He told me to keep the wound open until the ulcer healed. That way it would heal from the inside out, and by the time the skin healed, Spike would be ready for duty. I thanked him and said that I would never have thought of silver nitrate, that it wasn't taught in school anymore. Everything was supposed to be cured with the new sulfa drugs. (Today they say similar things about antibiotics, and knowledge learned firsthand is too often ignored.)

I thanked Dr. Boyce enthusiastically and asked if he would not please accept something for his time.

He would not. Forget it, he said, there wouldn't be any bill.

Dr. Boyce was the kind of veterinarian I hoped to one day become.

When we got back to camp, Colonel Parsons was waiting in the fire barn. He peered into the back of the recon and asked about the dog. Thanks to Dr. Boyce, I reported, everything would be fine. I told Parsons we'd operated on Spike's leg, drained the pus and cauterized an ulcer on his femur.

Then Colonel Parsons subjected me to another tirade. What "dumb ass," he wondered, would let an outfit like this ship out without any medical supplies when they had somebody that knew how to use them. He didn't care if I was a line officer; I was also a veterinarian and by God I was going to take care of these dogs. He handed me a pink piece of paper and asked again if I had any idea how much money the Corps had invested in each handler and dog. Timidly, I said I didn't. But he hadn't stopped yelling long enough to hear anything. Counting all facilities, transportation, housing and so forth, the cost of each dog was about $50,000.

The tirade continued, and Parsons shook his finger in my face as if I was the cause of it all. He warned me in no uncertain terms that the investment must be protected. Then for a moment his eyes relaxed and a look of compassion came over his old face. "Son, I don't want you to let any of these dogs die for want of anything we can provide." His face squeezed into wrinkles as if the brain controlling it had given way to some inner weakness that should have remained locked up. The redness returned and his angry mouth bellowed, "Would you do that much for me?"

"Yes, sir. I promise I will," I bellowed back at him. He glowered at me until he was sure I had gotten his point, then stomped to his jeep.

Only then did I look at the pink slip the colonel had given me. It authorized the holder to draw any supplies or equipment from any naval medical supply depot in the world. I told Hamilton to set up one of the supply tents for a dog sick bay. Tomorrow we would go to the medical supply depot and draw everything they had that we could use. From now on, we were in the veterinary business for both platoons.

By nightfall, Hamilton had erected the tent and painted and nailed to the center pole a sign that read

---

1ST WAR DOG FIELD HOSPITAL

LT. WM. W. PUTNEY, VETERINARIAN

★ CHAPTER FOUR ★

THE DOG MEN

The Raiders, our new camp mates, were an elite subset of the U.S. Marine Corps. A Raider officer serving as an observer with the Chinese Communist Army of Mao Tse-tung admired the Chinese so much that he adopted the slogan "Gung Ho" for the Raiders.

Many officers of the Raider Battalion were veterans of overseas duty and combat; some, for example, had participated in the raid on Makin Island, an incursion into the Japanese-held Marshall and Gilbert Islands in 1942. From a submarine offshore, these Raiders had paddled their boats onto the beach, where they destroyed the Japanese garrison and a communications base. Unfortunately, the Japanese had radioed that they were under attack before the radio tower was destroyed, and the Raiders were forced to return to their submarine and scamper below when Japanese Zeros burst onto the scene. Only a crash dive saved the day.

Needless to say, both Taylor and myself were quite impressed to be in the company of men who had seen combat in such a glorious and spectacular fashion. The Raiders, however, were not impressed by the war dog platoons. Nor were their rivals, the Paratroopers, elite troops trained to jump from airplanes into enemy territory and fight as infantry, who were stationed across the road.

One morning, Taylor and I visited the kennel area. The dogs' crates were lined up as directed and the dogs securely tethered to their stakes and chains. They had never been on chains before, but they seemed not to mind. Pfc. Al Tesch's Tippy, an Alaskan Husky that had come with the original group of dogs from the Army, was curled up on top of his crate just like an Arctic sled dog. The men were in formation and Barnowsky was giving them their instructions for the day when a six-by-six truck loaded with Paratroopers sped by. Spotting the dogs, the Paratroopers began making catcalls.

Evidently, there was a big rivalry going on between the Raiders and the parachute Marines that included sneaking into each other's camps in the middle of the night, stealing anything they could grab, and then cutting the tent ropes on sleeping Marines and laughing like crazy while the surprised men struggled to get out from underneath the canvas mess. The ostensible purpose of these nighttime raids was to show what lousy security their rivals had—if the Paratroopers could sneak up on the Raiders (or vice versa), so could the Japanese. The real purpose of those attacks was to humiliate their rivals, and both Raiders and Paratroopers afterward sent notes to rub it in.

With that in mind, Taylor ordered Barnowsky to post men with their dogs around our camp and capture any Paratroopers that tried to invade. He also ordered him to return any infiltrating Paratroopers to their camp under guard of a handler and his dog.

The war dog platoons had expected to be readily accepted into the Raider Battalion as full-fledged warriors, but the Paratroopers made that impossible. They heckled any Raiders who showed signs of friendliness toward the dog men, as they dubbed us, by making obscene remarks, and barking, scratching and howling. They threw hot dogs at the Raiders' camp and generally made complete fools of themselves.

The Raiders, in turn, took it out on the dog men. They resented our presence and made it known over and over. The mess sergeant sent the dog men to the rear of the chow line and most of the time they ended up with food that was cold—and little of it. It had taken us six months to instill some pride in our men, and they didn't deserve the treatment they were getting. I wanted to speak to Major Antonelli about it, but didn't want to appear to be whining. I needn't have worried. Two events occurred that put the matter to rest.

The first happened in the mess hall. The dog men were sent to the end of the chow line as usual and consequently were the last to be fed. We had worked hard that day and had missed our noon meal in an effort to get our camp squared away. The men had not been able to shower because a practical-joking Raider had cut the water off and the dog men, still new in camp, didn't know where the valve for the main pipe was located. They were tired and dirty and in no mood to have childish tricks played on them.

When my men got to the chow lines, the food was cold and the mess crew was dishing out half rations. They arrived at their designated tables and sat down amid snickers and catcalls. Then one of the Raiders cupped his hands over his mouth and let out a shrill and loud "Arrf . . . Arrf!" The rest of the Raiders howled in laughter.

Dog handler Pfc. Freddie Voight slowly put down his knife and fork. The massive six-foot four-inch Norwegian rose and calmly confronted the heckler by grabbing the lapels of his jacket, lifting him smoothly over his head and depositing him in the middle of a mess table—two rows back. The table's legs collapsed and dishes, food, and Raiders were scattered all over the floor.

The 110 dog men rose and stood shoulder-to-shoulder facing several hundred Raiders. The dog men would not win if a fight occurred, but the Raiders seemed to realize, for the first time, that they might give a good accounting of themselves. A gunnery sergeant yelled "At ease," and the confrontation was over. The

Raiders, in a rare display of graciousness, raised their canteen cups in a salute to Voight.

From that day forward, no Raider ever ridiculed a dog man again.

★   ★   ★

The Paratroopers learned a similar lesson a few days later. Just as we expected, they tried to raid the dog platoons' camp. Early one morning, Taylor and I were walking toward the dog area when a jeep suddenly roared down the company street between the two rows of tents. A lieutenant colonel jumped out and began screaming for the officer in charge. From twenty-five yards away, we could see from the colonel's red and flushed face that he was livid. Before his feet hit the ground, Barnowsky and Hamilton, who had heard the commotion, bounced out of the headquarters tent and ran to meet him.

He bellowed that he was CO of the Parachute Battalion and wanted to know who was in charge. Barney, who had just arrived, pointed to Bill Taylor.

Taylor asked what the trouble was. The colonel said that two of our men and their dogs woke him in the middle of the night; as he came out of his tent, he was met by a snarling, charging Doberman Pinscher—one of our men and his dog were herding about eight of his men.

Taylor said he was "astonished." He asked if the colonel's men had been in the dog platoons' camp. The colonel yelled that he didn't know whether they were or not, but the point was that they had been disrespectful to him and he wasn't going to have it. He said he wanted those two bastards with the dogs up for summary court. After they've been on bread and water for ten days, they would think twice about insulting a Marine colonel. Could the colonel identify them? Taylor asked.

The colonel could not identify them—it was pitch-dark, after all—but one of them, he said, muttered something to his dog in a foreign language.

Taylor did not think that would help: we had men that spoke all kinds of foreign languages. He glanced at me and continued that he, too, would not tolerate disrespectful conduct toward officers. If the man responsible was found, the colonel would be notified immediately and disciplinary measures taken.

When the angry colonel walked away, Taylor, finally letting the smile he had suppressed break out, told me the story. An old gunnery sergeant named Transport had warned some of the dog men that the Paratroopers would be trying to raid our camp, and Barney had ordered six men to walk their posts with their dogs. If anyone was spotted, the dog men were to withdraw quietly back into camp and notify him. Under no circumstances were they to challenge anyone.

Pfc. Adamski, an amateur boxer from Chicago, had been walking his post with Big Boy down by the creek behind our camp when the dog alerted. Adamski made certain that men were approaching before waking Barney, who had assigned one man from each squad with their dogs to quietly take up their positions according to our plan. The intruders sneaked into our camp and came down the company street thinking they had caught the dog men completely off guard. Just as they were about to cut some tent ropes, Barney blew his whistle and yelled for them to halt.

Instead, they bolted for the rear of the tents where the dogs met them head-on, straining at their leashes. Never before had so many stopped so quickly when faced with so few. The Paratroopers never knew what hit them. But when they turned to run back the way they had come, they ran right into Butch, going berserk. Schaible yelled (for dramatic effect) that he couldn't hold the dog much longer, and the men and dogs closed in on the hapless Paratroopers until they were herded into a small bunch. They pleaded for the dogs to be called off and were told to shut up and fall into a single file. Schaible turned Butch loose on one side and Allen Jacobson—an ex–star athlete from Baltimore, Maryland, bulky and six feet plus—let Kurt loose on the other.

Schaible had made them count cadence loud and clear right up to the colonel's tent.

★   ★   ★

Word got around camp that the war dog people had captured a squad of Paratroopers attempting to sneak into their camp. In all the months that the Raiders and the Paratroopers had been playing games, nobody had actually captured anybody. Scuttlebutt began that maybe there was something to the use of dogs after all. If the dogs could detect the approach of the Paratroopers, then there was no reason why they couldn't detect the approach of Japanese attempting to infiltrate Marine lines at night.

Gradually, some of the Raiders began to hang around the dog camp. They watched the dogs go through their basic obedience work and were amazed at the dogs' ability to keep up with the handlers during close order drill. Occasionally, Barnowsky had Schaible or Benny Goldblatt break out Butch or Peppy for an attack session. One of our sergeants, Orlando Maiorana, put on the padded rubber sleeve, and Butch and Peppy jumped at him, their handlers making it look even worse than it really was by encouraging the dogs to "eat him alive."

Sergeant Maiorana was a powerful, muscular man. But struggle as he might, he could not dislodge Butch once the dog had taken hold of his arm. As soon as Schaible yelled "Out," however, Butch let go and assumed a sitting position. But he never took his eyes off the hated sleeve. Once he had an attacker down, Peppy would straddle the man, glowering. No man ever made a move once Peppy was astride him; to do so would have been to invite disaster.

The Raiders were so impressed that they constantly asked for the attack demonstration.

We also demonstrated the dogs' exceptional sense of hearing. I told Bob Dowell to have some of his men gather down by the dog camp one afternoon so Barnowsky could show them how well the dogs could hear. Barney used a silent whistle to demonstrate Spike's acute sense of hearing. When Barney blew on the whistle, the men standing within a few feet could hear—barely—the sound of his breath filling it. The whistle's higher decibels, however, were inaudible to them but could be heard for great distances by the dogs.

To prove this point, Barney called Johnson and Spike out of the ranks and told Johnson to take Spike across the road with a couple of Raiders. Spike had a long crop so it would be easy to see him prick up his tall ears from quite a distance. Barney told Johnson to move up the hill about twenty yards at a time and for the Raiders to raise their arms if they could hear the whistle.

Johnson and Spike went across the road, stopped and turned around. Barney blew the whistle. Spike pricked up his ears at the sound and all the men held up their arms. Barney signaled Johnson to go another twenty yards up the hill. This time when Barney blew the whistle, only Spike could hear it. The entourage moved another twenty yards up the hill, and Spike responded to the whistle again. When they had gone one hundred and twenty yards up the hill, Spike continued to respond. Barney held up his arm and motioned for Johnson and Spike to move on. Finally, at 180 yards up the hill, Barney blew on the whistle and Spike just sat still. He had reached the limit of his ability to hear the whistle.

Dogs, Barney explained, hear much better at night than in the daytime. Their ears are working even when they are sleeping. They don't sleep with one eye open, so to speak, but with both ears perked. Dogs, he said, usually do not respond to sounds that are familiar to them—a family dog, after all, does not usually bark when a family member comes to the door. The dog recognizes the difference in smell, or in the noise made by the footsteps of the intruders.

Barney told the Raiders that we would be going on maneuvers with them. They should not be alarmed if the handler walked his dog among them—the handler would just be letting his dog know who was family.

★　★　★

By now we had gained the respect of Tent Camp 2, and the men began to think of ways to make the most of it. I noticed Pfc. Arthur Spielman and his dog Bunkie watching our demonstrations carefully—too carefully, it seemed to me. I grew even more suspicious when I saw Spielman, on his own time, taking Bunkie out beyond the camp's perimeter.

Spielman was a product of New York City's Hell's Kitchen, a far tougher neighborhood in the 1940s than it is today. Intelligent and inquisitive, Spielman never did anything without thinking about it beforehand. Usually, he was thinking about how he could make a buck out of it. This is not to say that he was a bad Marine; he was one of the best men I had.

Spielman's dog, Bunkie, was trained as a messenger dog. He was a very small gray and black German Shepherd with large ears and had an unusual characteristic: when the other dogs were all sitting at attention, little Bunkie usually sat up with his front legs off the ground like a prairie dog, so he would be as tall as the others.

As a messenger dog, Bunkie had two handlers: Spielman and Pfc. William Harper, the second-youngest man in the outfit (Spielman was the youngest). Coming from Corpus Christi, Harper became known as Tex. Harper and Spielman were always together, the Texan constantly being fed advice by the far worldlier Spielman. I questioned Tex, but he confessed to total ignorance of Spielman's current venture.

The next Saturday afternoon it all became clear. Behind the supply tent Sergeant Hamilton saw Spielman giving a lecture to a group of Raiders on Bunkie's discerning sense of smell. He demonstrated by sending Bunkie to retrieve a marked stone from a pile of similar rocks. After several of these demonstrations, Spielman went so far as to proclaim that Bunkie could find any particular stone in a pile that he asked for and return it. His audience of Raiders did not believe him—just as Spielman had hoped.

Spielman said that he would prove it: Bunkie could retrieve any stone that he was told to, and Spielman would bet them a dollar a man that Bunkie would never pick up the wrong rock.

A platoon sergeant offered to hold the pot. He took off his cap and passed it around, and it returned with twenty-two dollars. Spielman reached into his pocket and pulled out two crumpled tens and two ones and handed them over to the platoon sergeant. He asked the men to get their stones and mark them and hang on to them until they told him which stone they wanted Bunkie to retrieve.

The Raiders scrambled all over the creek bed and returned with their stones. They passed a pencil around and marked each. Spielman went down the line and asked that the man who had the stone to be retrieved hold up his hand. A burly Marine named Hank held up his stone, and Spielman held it aloft for them all to inspect. Did they agree that he held the stone that they wanted? They did. He handed it back to Hank and all of them took their stones to the platoon sergeant and dropped them into his hat.

Spielman told the sergeant to shake and throw them. The sergeant shook the cap and threw the stones as far as he could, scattering them all over the area. The Raiders laughed, thinking they had pulled a fast one on the dog man.

But Spielman paid no attention. He put Bunkie at the heel position and leaned down and whispered loudly into his ear to fetch Hank's stone. He unleashed the little Shepherd, who bounded in the direction of the scattered stones. Bunkie began the tedious task of visiting each stone lying around on the ground. He sniffed stone after stone and abandoned one after another. He had visited at least half of the stones when he suddenly put his mouth down, grabbed one, and returned. Spielman reached down and took the stone out of his mouth. He called Hank over and handed it to him.

Hank took the stone in his hand and examined it, turning it over and over. Gradually, a look of defeat came over his face. He felt that there was some kind of trick being played on him. Maybe Spielman had palmed the stone and had it in his pocket all the time?

The platoon sergeant entered the controversy and said he'd kept his eye on Spielman all the time: he had won the money fair and square. But Hank argued that these slick guys from New York had all kinds of tricks. He challenged Spielman to go again; this time, however, he was going to hold the stone until he gave it to the sergeant.

Spielman looked like he had just been caught. He frowned and looked down at Bunkie. He raised his head and, almost in a whisper, agreed reluctantly to repeat the exercise. The sergeant gathered the money again while the men regathered their stones. A small, red-headed Marine held up his stone, gave it to Spielman and asked for the dog to find it.

Spielman took the stone and said he wanted to examine the mark to make sure that he'd recognize it. He examined it and returned it to the Raider, who looked at it again and confirmed that it was indeed his—Spielman had not palmed it.

"Okay, send him out," said the sergeant as he threw their stones.

Spielman leaned over Bunkie and said in a pleading whisper, "Bunkie, you gotta do your best. If you can't do it, we'll still be friends, but try your best." Bunkie looked up at Spielman earnestly. Spielman unleashed him, and, in a weak voice, told him to fetch.

Bunkie trotted out and began sniffing the stones. He examined stone after stone, returning to some he'd already smelled. He sniffed one stone three times.

"Make sure, Bunkie, make sure," exhorted Spielman.

Finally, Bunkie picked up a different stone in his mouth and returned to the heel position beside his master. Spielman reached down and extracted the stone and with a look of uncertainty gave it to the redheaded Marine, who gasped. It was his stone.

Spielman gave a sigh of relief, took the money from the sergeant, and sent the Raiders back to their part of the camp. When they were gone, Hamilton came over to Spielman. "You really screwed them guys," he said.

"What do you mean, Sergeant?"

"I saw you send Bunkie back to those stones he'd already smelled by using arm and hand signals. Bunkie obeyed, but he knew that they weren't the ones."

Spielman smiled and said he didn't have the slightest idea what Hamilton was talking about—Bunkie had just gotten lucky.

"That's probably the biggest lie I've ever heard," muttered Hamilton.

Spielman never told Sergeant Hamilton—who was not a dog trainer—the secret. All Spielman had to do was to put his fingertip on the stone and Bunkie's sense of smell was so acute that he would never miss no matter where Spielman sent him with hand signals.

Spielman, ebullient, returned to his tent and announced to Tex Harper: "I got forty bucks. Get your greens on and let's ask Hamilton if we can go to town."

★　★　★

Major Antonelli called Taylor and me into the office to tell us we would join his troops in a night exercise against the Paratroopers. We'd worked the dogs in offensive and defensive positions among ourselves and were extremely pleased with the results, but it was critical to find out how well they would work with strange troops under conditions that best simulated combat.

He laid out the scenario for the exercise: the Raider Battalion with dog troops would have (fictitiously) landed on the beach five miles below San Onofre and proceeded about two miles inland. The Paratroop Battalion would act as a hostile force defending against our invasion and would launch a counterattack against our position. They would attempt to destroy the Raider Battalion and, in so doing, repulse our landing and theoretically drive the remains of us back into the sea.

Antonelli wanted to win this exercise in the worst way, and, after hearing of the dog men's run-in with the CO of the Parachute Battalion, he was impressed with our dogs' abilities. I further assured him that we had trained hard to acquire the skills that would be valuable under just such circumstances.

The Raiders would be defending a ridge above a small, dirty stream called Hansen's Creek in the northern sector of Camp Pendleton. I would be attached to Able Company on the right, Taylor to Charlie Company on the left and Baker Company would be held in reserve. The map displayed by the CO showed terrain beyond the edge leveling off for a distance of about four hundred yards, then rising sharply to two hills. In the center between the hills, the ground was fairly level. According to the rules, the attack must come between Point A, at the extreme right of Hill 304, and Point B, at the extreme left of Hill 287. We were to be in position and dug in by 1800 hours.

Major Antonelli briefed his officers, along with Taylor and me, and explained that the dogs would be used for the first time in one of these operations. It was my job to explain to Antonelli's men what to expect from them. The Corps, I explained, planned to use the dogs in combat as an early-warning system to give us valuable time to prepare before an attack. The dogs would remain silent, regardless of what might happen; under no circumstances would they bark and give away our position.

On this maneuver, we would have a dog and handler in each of the machine-gun positions and one on the right flank of the company. We would be able to warn of the coming attack long enough in advance to eliminate any chance of surprise.

As we were leaving, I asked Taylor which of the men he would be using. He said he would use Baldwin in the company command post, Dickerson and Pal, Carl Bliss and Hobo, and Thurman Clark and Duke. I chose Dentino for the company command post, and Marvin

Corff and Rocky, Allen Jacobson and Kurt, and Ed Adamski and Big Boy. We felt these six dogs and handlers were among our best.

Taylor had mixed emotions about the maneuver, but I felt that it would be a good chance to show our superiors what we could do. The time of testing was soon upon us. By 1800 hours on the evening of the exercise, the Raider Battalion was dug in along the ridge. The Battalion front spread five hundred yards from flank to flank. The men were relaxing in their foxholes, and the battalion command post was a hubbub of friendly chatter as the radios to Able and Charlie Companies were checked and rechecked. Major Antonelli asked Taylor if the dogs and men were ready.

Taylor said they were briefed and checked into their positions and had been turned over to their company commanders. Sergeant Dentino was with Able Company and Sergeant Baldwin was with Charlie Company.

The major asked if it was Vincent Dentino. It turned out that the major knew him; Dentino had been his runner when he was a Pfc. Dentino was a small, sneaky guy from the Bronx. The major smiled fondly and said that unless he had changed, he would make us a fine sergeant. Dentino could sneak his way through a whole regiment of troops without anyone even knowing he was around and walked so silently it was eerie. Dentino should be careful, though, the major warned, and snap his fingers when he came within earshot of fellow Marines in combat, or one day he might surprise somebody that was jumpy. In fact, I had noticed Dentino snapping his fingers when he approached me, but I had always figured he was just nervous.

When Dentino arrived at Able Company, he placed his men in their assigned foxholes and gave them instructions. In the last few minutes of daylight, he walked the entire length of the company front and noticed a small ditch that ran from the ridge starting at the point on the right side of A Company's position, down the hill and into the creek bed. The ditch was only about two and a half feet deep and three to four feet wide at the widest point. Only about two men at a time could use the ditch for cover if they wanted to infiltrate A Company's position. He called Jacobson and told him to dig in at the top of the ditch.

Allen Jacobson tied Kurt to a bush and unsheathed his trenching tool. Jake, as he was known, had a constant smile on his face. He was one of the favorites of the men.

"Dig it deep enough for me, too," said Dentino. "I'll be spending the night with you." On the extreme right flank of the battalion, in the outermost exposed position, Pfc. Corff and his Doberman, Rocky, occupied a foxhole with a heavy .30-caliber machine gun. A foxhole to their left contained two riflemen whose job was to prevent any enemy from crawling close enough to toss a grenade into the emplacement.

If the machine-gun emplacement was destroyed, the entire flank of the battalion could be overrun. The guns were placed in such a manner that in addition to being able to fire straight ahead, they could fire across the front of the position, overlapping with the field of fire of the machine guns down the line, and covering, together, the entire front. This was a standard Marine Corps defense—and one the Paratroopers would expect.

Corff was a quiet, intelligent twenty-three-year-old who had grown up on a farm in Illinois. He was eating from a can of C rations with the blade of his K-Bar knife when Sergeant Dentino approached, and he held up the can of rations and cheerily invited Dentino to join him for dinner. All he got was a frown, so Corff emptied the remaining contents of the can in front of Rocky. The big

Doberman would have none of it. He took one sniff, lifted his leg to relieve himself on the "Beef and Vegetable Stew," and flopped down on the ground facing in the opposite direction.

"Even the dog has more sense than to eat that stuff," chuckled one of the machine-gunners.

There was a ditch just to the left of the machine-gun emplacement on the other side of the company, and Dentino would be at its head. If Corff suspected anybody approaching from his side, he was to call the other machine-gun section immediately. Dentino wanted a compass reading of the direction of the approach so it could be plotted on the situation map.

Pfc. Ben Dickerson lay on the ground staring into the darkness ahead, with Pal curled up on a pile of dirt in front of his foxhole. Pal stirred occasionally, pricked up his ears, turned his head into the wind, sniffed and then lay back down. The night was black and still; only a slight breeze blew in from the southwest. The Raider position was directly downwind from the expected direction of attack—perfect for our dogs. Occasionally, a coyote on a distant hill let out a howl and was answered by one of his kind farther up the mountain. The war dogs had by now become accustomed to the call of their wild cousins in the hills surrounding their camp and had ceased to react to them at all.

At exactly 1836, Pal stood, sniffed into the wind, and pricked up his ears again. Dickerson moved to his side as Pal let out an almost inaudible growl. The hackles on his neck rose and he froze in a position pointing to the right. Dickerson pulled out his compass and sighted in the direction Pal was pointing. He snapped the lid shut and told the sergeant that he could report a definite alert at an azimuth 135 degrees. The sergeant asked if Dickerson was sure.

Dickerson replied that he was supposed to tell the sergeant the minute he knew someone was approaching his position. Now he knew someone was approaching, so the sergeant should call the CP, the command post. Otherwise, Dickerson would go back to camp where it was warm.

The sergeant picked up the field telephone, gave the handle a crank, and reported the approach.

When I received word, I spread my shelter half on the ground and crawled underneath, extracted my map of the area from its case and flipped on my flashlight. With a protractor I drew a line on the map, exactly along the azimuth given to me.

Somebody kicked my feet. It was Taylor; he had just gotten an alert from Baldwin, who said that Bliss gave him an azimuth of 230 degrees.

I plotted the latest information on the map. Where the two lines intersected, I made a circle. The distance from its center to the battalion line was about 750 yards, or almost a half-mile. That was where we would find the advancing party.

Taylor asked if I would be willing to bet the outcome of the whole exercise on it. Before I could answer, the telephone clicked again. It was Baldwin: Duke had just alerted straight ahead.

Taylor called the main command post and told the major that we had spotted the enemy entering the draw on the far side between the two hills.

During the next thirty minutes, the reports from the forward positions continued, each report further substantiating previous ones. The advancing column was now identified and located beyond any doubt. Then the reports ceased. The dogs, having done their duty, seemed to be resting on their laurels.

But something was odd. If the column was moving toward us, the dogs should be becoming more agitated, not going to sleep. I checked with Baldwin and Dentino again and was informed that everything was quiet, the dogs were resting, and there were no further alerts. I came to the only conclusion that seemed possible; the column had stopped. I checked my azimuths of the last solid alerts; the front of the column must be resting near the entrance to the draw, about 550 yards from the forward line of the Raider Battalion.

I passed the information we had along to the manuever's umpire, so that we would have a record we could refer to later. The umpire recorded that the enemy had been spotted at 1836 at the far entrance of the draw and that during the next forty-five minutes they had moved to the near entrance and now remained stationary.

The phone began to click again, with Dentino reporting that Pal was on the alert. Dickerson was unable to tell if there had been a change in our opponents' positions. I looked at my watch: 1951. Five minutes later, Baldwin gave a similar report. Hobo was on the alert now, but if the enemy was moving, the direction could not be determined.

Dentino reported that the compass reading of Rocky's alerting was increasing. The invading force was moving to the right. He also reported that the dog was not terribly disturbed, meaning that they were not approaching closer. They could only be moving lateral to the battalion front line.

But this conclusion, which seemed the only explanation possible, was shattered when Baldwin reported that Pal was alerting and that he was pointing more and more to the left. What's going on? I wondered. I picked up the phone and asked Dentino if he was sure of Corff's reading of Rocky.

He was sure. Kurt was pointing increasingly to the right; the Paratroopers were moving in that direction. I told Dentino that Dickerson was sure they were moving to the left.

A thought crossed my mind. I asked if Dentino thought the Paratroopers might be splitting their forces and moving toward both flanks.

It was possible. There was a brief silence and Dentino said Rocky was pointing straight ahead.

After our conversation, Dentino sat in the dark on the side of the foxhole and mulled over the situation. He pushed himself over the side of the foxhole, crawled into the ditch and began to make his way toward the creek bed. Moving stealthily in a crouch, he avoided every outcropping of rock and bush as he navigated the three-foot ditch.

When he arrived at the creek bed, it was empty. But after moving to his left about a hundred yards, the silence was broken by the sound of muffled voices. He was within fifteen yards of a group of men huddled in the creek bed and saw more figures moving from the rear into it.

From the muted sound of canteens brushing against bushes and the shuffling of feet, he determined that a column of men was moving into the creek bed and spreading out along its bottom. He remembered Gunny Holdren's continual warning about the weakness of the flanks of an entrenched position and the consequent necessity of protecting them.

To Sergeant Vincent Dentino, the picture was clear. The Paratroopers were using the creek bed as a staging area. When all of their troops were in place, the attack would begin. He thought about what the dogs had been trying to tell him, but not until now had he understood their message. As the dogs indicated, the enemy had regrouped after emerging from the draw and began to move to both sides in order to attack the Raiders' two flanks simultaneously. The only thing left for him to do before returning to his foxhole was to confirm his theory.

He began to move back down the creek bed. With the Paratroopers consumed by the intricacies of their own staging, they did not expect him in their vicinity, and he walked cautiously but swiftly around their position.

He passed the place where the ditch emptied into the creek bed and proceeded until he could hear the rustle of men entering the sandy bottom and flopping against the bank. Silently, he approached to within fifteen paces of them. Once he determined that the rear end of the column was entering the creek bed, he had no need to stay longer.

He turned away from the enemy and toward the ditch. When he was far enough away not to be heard, he broke into a soundless run. He made his way up the ditch, called the password to the machine-gun outpost, and clamored into the foxhole with Jacobson and Kurt. He called me from the machine-gunner's telephone and explained that the Paratroopers were staging an attack on both flanks and were ready to jump off any minute. They had split their forces; the attack would come on both flanks.

I rushed to the other side of the CP and told the major that we had firsthand confirmation of the dogs' warnings. They could attack any minute.

That's good enough for me, he said. He reached for a field telephone and turned the crank. He told the weapons company to give him a flare in front of his position in two minutes. They were to lay down a (pretend) barrage on the creek bed the moment the flare went off. He informed the umpire and told him to be sure that his times and locations were accurate. The Paratroopers would be slaughtered.

The first flare went off, and all across the battalion front the machine guns went up with a constant clatter. Their blank ammunition made a series of yellow and red flashes as the powder exploded in their barrels and red-hot wadding flew out the ends. Down in the creek bed, in the light of the flare, men could be seen trying to hide against the near bank. Some were scrambling to the rear. Others stood frozen in an effort not to be observed. Ten minutes later he told his executive officer to give the cease-fire order. The front fell into silence.

It was ruled that the attacking force had been caught in the open and 90 percent destroyed. A check of the umpire's times and plotted positions revealed that the first alert by Pal at six thirty-six had been accurate. The position of the attacking force was confirmed by Rocky and Hobo—at a distance of 720 yards. When the force split, it was still 420 yards away.

When we arrived back at camp, we reported to the rest of the men what had taken place on our first outing with troops other than our own. Barney was ecstatic; he could hardly believe that the dogs picked up people almost a half-mile away.

The successful exploits of the war dogs spread throughout Camp Pendleton and erased whatever animosity lingered between the Raiders and the dog men. The commanding general even paid a visit and watched with fascination as the dogs put on a show. Hollywood and Pathé News, fascinated by the dogs as always, sent a camera crew and a director from *Time Marches On,* the most popular newsreel shown in theaters across the country, to shoot the dogs in action. The director at first wanted to tie bayonets to the backs of the dogs, ridiculous as it seems, with the points sticking out over their heads, preferably emerging from landing craft and charging some beach on an anonymous Pacific island. His vision of war dogs seemed to be of vicious animals, their jaws hanging open, and fangs exposed, and ready to bayonet and devour a treacherous enemy.

Taylor and I would not have it. We tried in vain to explain to the director that if he would just let us show him what the dogs could do and what they were trained for, it would be a good—maybe even great—show, far better than the wildest fiction he could devise. We could not change his mind, though, and finally refused to cooperate until the matter was decided elsewhere. After calls from the studio head in Hollywood, Colonel Parsons intervened and told the director in typical Marine Corps style to either shoot it the way the war dog officers want it or not at all.

That ended the matter and the scenes were shot just as we had initially insisted. They were far better than anybody expected, including the director, who said, "Why didn't you tell me the dogs could perform on cue like that? I could use some of them at the studio."

"I'm sure some of them will be looking for work after the war," I said. "But you'll have to talk to their agents."

CHAPTER FIVE

THE LAST DAYS AT CAMP PENDLETON

The Raiders left for the Northern Boundary Camp at San Clemente, a larger town near San Onofre, about ten days after our exercises, and Colonel Parsons said he was sending out a mess sergeant and some cooks for our mess hall. The Raiders had left a $7,000 surplus in the mess account with the commissary, and we would inherit it. It didn't surprise me. Their mess sergeant had fed them the worst chow in camp. There was an allowance of 28 cents per man per day and mess sergeants are supposed to handle their accounts so as to come out even at the end of each month. But mess sergeants that saved money got points at the commissary, and points at the commissary could be used by an unscrupulous sergeant who was bucking for a promotion.

Because I was a veterinarian (and thus better versed in nutritional requirements than anyone else), Colonel Parsons said that I would become the mess officer—in addition to serving as CO—of one of the war dog platoons. I would have to fall back on my old food inspection classes.

Taylor laughed and said I'd better get cracking with the books; the colonel would be out to inspect the mess hall the next Saturday. I asked him if he thought the colonel knew anything about the mess account surplus.

"No," he said, "I don't think he's interested."

"From here on," I warned, "as long as we are here alone, I'm going to use every damn penny of that surplus, even if we have to eat steak every day."

I tried my best, but I failed. In spite of having steak, oysters, strawberries that were not in season, and ice cream, we were never able to use all of the money in the account even though the word got around about the wonderful food at the dog camp and we were deluged with visitors.

The U.S. Marine Corps, like the Army, is a place of feast or famine. It's a wonderful place, but one in which you had to look out for yourself to get by. Common sense would dictate that certain things—like weapons, for example—would be so essential that the Corps could not possibly afford to place Marines at risk by the issuance of imperfect weapons. Common sense would be wrong.

We were issued 115 M-1 carbines in Camp Pendleton in place of the standard .45-caliber automatic pistols. The weapon, a small semiautomatic rifle, had a magazine that held fifteen rounds of .30-caliber ammunition. The Corps apparently felt that the heavier Garand, standard issue for riflemen, was too bulky for a dog handler to carry while working his dog on a leash. (They did not know that we were training our handlers to work their dogs off-leash.) Within two hours of their arrival, Taylor and I were handed our carbines all cleaned, oiled and ready to use.

Taylor asked Hamilton where the ammunition was kept. I'm going hunting, he said, and beckoned me to follow.

Every afternoon about four o'clock, a flock of ducks circled and landed about a quarter of a mile up on the hill behind our camp. The ducks apparently were landing on a small pond, just out of the line of sight from the camp. Taylor said that if we climbed up the hill, nearly to the pond, and then crawled the rest of the way, we could shoot enough ducks for the mess sergeant to cook duck dinner for the whole outfit.

When we were within fifty yards of what we figured was the site of the pond, we began to crawl. Gradually, the pond came into view. Covering its surface were over a hundred mallards, canvasbacks and mud hens. We crawled forward until the whole flock of ducks sensed our presence and scrambled across the water and took off. I opened fire on a large mallard drake—and missed every feather. A hen followed him closely and I let go with two shots in rapid succession. She never turned. I turned and fired at ducks and even mud hens until my fifteen-round clip was exhausted. I missed every single one.

Shamefully, I asked Taylor how many he got. "Not a damned one," he replied. I told him I was glad none of the men were here to see our exhibition of marksmanship.

We reloaded and, for amusement, began to fire at several beer cans that were floating on the pond. We missed the cans by one or two feet. Taylor wondered what had happened to him. He had made expert rifleman on the range at Parris Island.

When we arrived back in camp, Barnowsky saw we were empty-handed and chided us, "What did you two hunters bring back for dinner? I heard so much firing up there that if I hadn't known it was you two, I'd have sounded general quarters."

Taylor replied that Barney should grab a couple of carbines and come with us to the camp rifle range. There it became instantly clear that our rifles were so badly sighted that they could not hit a two-foot target at a hundred yards. What would happen to the men, we wondered, if they were put on point with a weapon like this?

The logical thing to do was to ask the camp's quartermaster for new rifles. But what would the quartermaster give us? The same mass-produced carbines that he had issued before. If we wanted to correct the situation, we would have to do it on our own.

Transport, the Raiders' gunnery sergeant, was an excellent gun-smith, and volunteered to help us. The carbines always shot low when they came from the factory, he said, but he could fix them by filing the front sight. If they shot high, there would be nothing he could do. With a file from his toolbox, he scraped at the front sight until the gun shot closer to the bull's-eye, but still almost a foot off. He continued filing and tapping on the rear sight until the shots were so tightly grouped in the bull's-eye that a silver dollar would cover them all. It took an hour and a half to correct four carbines.

Fixing ten carbines every Saturday afternoon would mean that it would take eleven weeks to repair the 111 that remained—and we were scheduled to ship out as soon as a vessel was available. Taylor asked him if Transport would work on them full-time.

Of course he would—but only if Taylor could get permission from the major. He didn't want our boys to go into combat with the rifles the way they were.

On Monday morning, the CO, having seen the work of the dogs on the night maneuver and knowing our need for accurate rifles, agreed to let Transport work on the carbines full-time for two weeks. He could have use of a jeep so he could return to the North-ern Boundary Camp every night.

This arrangement lasted one day. When Transport ate his first meal in our mess hall, he decided to stay the whole two weeks in Tent Camp 2. Two weeks later we thanked Transport, gave him a case of Mattingly & Moore, his favorite drink, and sent him on his way. All of our carbines would now group in a six-inch circle at two hundred yards.

★ ★ ★

The time remaining before we would receive our sailing orders was growing short. Within a day of the Raiders' departure for the main camp at Oceanside, twenty miles south, the Parachute Battalion had moved away. We were now all alone, in our own camp. That meant that the war dog platoons would take over military police duty in San Clemente. It would be our job to see that all Marines behaved themselves while on liberty in the seaside town.

This would be the first time the public would see Marine war dogs, and there would be a great deal of curiosity. I told the men not to let the dogs display any aggressiveness. Their presence alone, I was sure, would be deterrent enough to anyone who might contemplate creating a problem.

Sure enough, the dogs, which were beautifully groomed for their police work, drew large gatherings of civilians whenever they were on duty. People stopped the handlers and asked all sorts of questions about the dogs. Some were brave enough to ask if they could pet the dogs, but policy forbade this and they were not allowed to do so.

Within a few days, a tradition had begun. As soon as the dogs appeared on duty, onlookers hurried to Reilly's Café to buy hamburgers, which they offered to the handlers to feed to the dogs. The dogs made out well, while the Marines exploited the situation to get the addresses or telephone numbers of girls that took an interest in the animals.

This continued until we shipped out and, in my opinion, San Clemente under the patrol of the war dog platoons was the quietest town on the West Coast. A single fight broke out between some sailors and visiting soldiers, but by the time our men arrived, the sailors had won and invited the soldiers and our MPs down to Reilly's Café for hotcakes, including sausage for the dogs.

During the same period, I found it necessary to replace three dogs, all Dobermans. Beau was found dead one morning. His belly was greatly distended and bloated. On autopsy, I found that he had torsion of the stomach. This is common in large dogs, and if not treated immediately, death results as the toxic gases formed by fermentation are absorbed from the stomach into the bloodstream.

After gorging on food and drinking a lot of water, the stomach becomes very heavy and floats awkwardly around in the abdomen like a large balloon inflated with a combination of solids and liquid. If the dog makes a quick move to turn over or jumps down from a high place such as a shipping crate, the dog turns but the stomach stays put. The result is a twist at the entrance and exit of the stomach. Gas produced by the digestion of the food or fermentation is trapped in the stomach, and unable to escape by belching or flatulence, the gas causes the stomach to distend. If the condition is not relieved by passing a tube through the mouth down to the stomach, or if surgery to open the stomach to release the gas does not effectively relieve the condition, the dog dies either from the absorption of the toxic gas, or rupture of the stomach. In this case, the distension took place during the night and Beau's condition unfortunately went undetected until the following morning.

One other dog needed to be returned to the War Dog Training School. Goth continually attacked his handler, Pfc. Ernest Childs from Casanova, Virginia. Because he was one of the oldest men—all of twenty-eight—the war dog Marines addressed Childs as "Uncle Joe." The last bite Uncle Joe Childs suffered was deep into the calf muscles on the rear of his leg, and was not healing well despite Childs's numerous trips to sick bay. Despite my reluctance to treat a human, I succumbed to his pleas for help, and after a few days of heat packs and sulfa, the leg began to heal. But Childs was not eager to go into combat with Goth.

"What about that dog, sir? He's bitten me four times before and this time it was serious. He's no good for combat. I've had dogs all my life and trained some of the best bird dogs in Fauquier County. But this dog is too dumb to be trained and he's mean as hell." I agreed, and decided to return the dog and find Childs a replacement before we shipped out.

The last dog that I wanted to replace had been trained as a messenger dog, but was so phlegmatic and sluggish that she slept almost all of the time. I examined her several times and could find no physical ailment, but clearly she would not be able to perform as a messenger dog—Cher Ami she wasn't—she was not even sharp enough to be used on night security. To keep her would deprive us of the use of two Marines (she had two handlers, like all the messenger dogs) and a dog when we got into combat. We needed every dog we could get, but each one had to be totally dependable.

I went to Colonel Parsons, who said he would contact Washington and let me know about replacements. Two days later he handed me a requisition form for three new dogs, which I was to pick up from Carl Spitz, owner of the Hollywood Dog Training School, and the one who had worked with the 1st Platoon before it went overseas. When I asked the colonel if Washington had specified what kind of dogs I was to get, he said no, I should get the best dogs Spitz had available.

Thursday morning, Tomaszewski loaded three crates into the recon and we headed for Hollywood. There, in an enclosed yard, a short, bald man about fifty years old was throwing small firecrackers around a black and tan German Shepherd that a handler was leading around a ring. The dog bolted against the leash each time a firecracker exploded. The handler pulled the dog back to his side and consoled him, softly offering some words of encouragement. But after three or four explosions, the dog began to shake, in spite of the positive reinforcement from the handler. He was led from the ring and deemed unacceptable for military duty because he was gun-shy.

Seeing me, the bald man—Spitz—approached and extended his hand. Having been with the 1st War Dog Platoon when they were at Pendleton, he wanted to know if I had heard anything from them.

I told him they had been in combat on Bougainville and, from the reports, they had performed admirably.

Spitz had brought ten Dobermans that had already passed all of their requirements to Hollywood especially for me, and began to run them through a battery of tests so that I might choose the three best of these. From Spitz, I recruited one Shepherd and one Doberman, and from a civilian boy, Bobby, I recruited Poncho, a fast, muscular Shepherd. Spitz told me he had another female Shepherd named Lady that had passed the induction requirements but was too skittish to make a scout dog. Her owner had refused to pay for her training and told Spitz to get rid of her. She was ours if I wanted her; Spitz thought I could use her as a messenger, or as a replacement, later.

I only had permission to recruit three dogs but I was confident Colonel Parsons would agree that we could keep her. Ski led all four dogs to our jeep, and after some difficulty with Lady, who was indeed quite jumpy, we left.

★   ★   ★

The return trip to Camp Pendleton was uneventful. We stopped near Orange, California, and took the dogs out for exercise. At first

Lady did not want to come out of the crate, but with a little coaxing she did, and when the leash was put on her collar, she obediently went with Ski and did her chores. There was no difficulty with the other dogs, and Poncho seemed to be thrilled with his Marine Corps experience.

When we arrived at San Clemente, I asked Ski to drop me off at the hotel where Taylor and I had taken a room. I told him to be sure to securely attach the dogs' chains to their stakes. We didn't want to lose any of them by having a clasp come loose.

I had just finished recounting the details of the trip to Taylor when the recon skidded to the curb out front. In a few minutes, there was a loud knock at the door. There stood one of the Marines in my platoon, Quillen, with his cap in his hand. He had been helping Ski with the dogs, he said, when Lady got away from them as they were taking her out of the crate. Lady had slammed into the crate door the moment it was unlatched, knocking him aside. They'd tried to catch her but she was too spooky. Barney had turned out all of the guys to search for her, but she couldn't be found in the dark.

I groaned but was relieved that the escapee was the extra one. We wouldn't have to report it. We would gather the men and conduct a full-scale search for Lady in the morning. With sunrise the search was on. I gave Barney instructions to have a pan of dog food put out every night in the center of the kennel area. If Lady came back to eat, he should have one of the men on guard duty watch to see where she went.

The food was put out each night for two nights—and taken back intact both nights. On the third night, Barney reported that one of the men on guard had heard Lady barking near the camp. Tomaszewski scouted around and found what he believed to be the spot in which she was spending her nights. On the following nights, she continued to come down from the hills for food but never exposed herself in the daytime.

I spiked the food with morphine, hoping that it would sedate her enough that we could walk over to her and pick her up. One effect that morphine has when given to dogs is that they often vomit shortly after ingesting it. The result is that though some dogs get narcotized in spite of the vomiting, most do not.

The chance of catching Lady with morphine was slim, but I tried it anyway. I added one half-grain of morphine to the food. We found her vomit next morning, but she evidently did not retain enough to drug her. I increased the dose to one grain and the same thing happened. I put two full grains into the food with no better results. (Dogs take a considerately higher dose of morphine for the same effects than do humans. One half-grain of morphine is an ample battlefield dose for a severely wounded man; the same amount is only a normal preanesthetic dose for a large dog, despite the size differential.) Morphine can be fatal in high doses to both man and dogs, and I didn't want to risk killing Lady by further increasing the dosage.

I turned to barbiturates instead. Nembutal is a long-lasting barbiturate that can be used as an anesthetic in dogs. It is usually injected but can also be used as a sleeping pill, so I laced several pieces of meat with Nembutal and left them for Lady to eat. For the first two nights, it rained and she ignored it. On the third day the rain was still coming down in torrents. On the following morning, with the weather finally dry, Tomaszewski arrived at the hotel earlier than usual. He reported that Lady was lying in front of her food pan. The Nembutal had totally sedated her; she was just lying there in the rain all covered with mud.

I pulled on my long johns and wool issue pants and a "peacoat," made by cutting down an enlisted man's overcoat to mid-thigh length. They were standard issue by the Navy, but not approved for us. Nevertheless, many Marine officers preferred peacoats because they were less bulky than regular overcoats.

Twenty minutes later we got to camp. Lady lay in the mud, just as Ski had said, as if fast asleep. I knew that she was alive because I could see her ribs rising and falling as she breathed heavily. Slowly, I approached her from behind and gradually moved my hands to a position above the nape of her neck. I intended to grasp her skin above her shoulder with my left hand and encircle her neck with my right arm (the best way to control a dog that might be dangerous). That way, no matter what her intentions, I would not be bitten.

The second I touched her, she bolted upright. I grabbed her by the hind legs. She made no attempt to bite, but as she struggled to escape, I lost my balance and she twisted away. The mud on her legs was so slippery that she was impossible to hold.

She stumbled around in the mud, half-crawling, half-walking, and scrambled toward San Onofre Creek. I slipped and slid after her, Ski at my side. She turned to her left and Ski went down in the mud trying to turn with her. We gained on her, but before we could make the capture, she plunged headlong into San Onofre Creek. I jumped in behind her and Ski plowed in right behind me.

The creek, normally only a few inches of stagnant water, was now eight feet deep and pouring toward the sea at fifteen or twenty miles an hour. There was no way I could swim or get my balance, and I was carried helplessly downstream, Lady floating about ten yards ahead of me and Ski floundering the same distance behind me. Luckily, my peacoat had captured a sufficient amount of air to act as a life vest.

We were powerless, carried by the violent river like little chips of wood. I called back to Ski to let the current take him downstream, not to fight it, just try to keep afloat.

He yelled that he was okay, and for me to take care of myself and forget about the dog.

That advice was not needed; there was nothing else I could do. All three of us were at the mercy of the raging water. Every twenty or thirty yards, the current would drag me underwater and the peacoat lifted me back to the surface.

Downstream about a quarter of a mile, the creek made a left turn. I could see the water whirling into the bank at the turn, and I also saw a large tree overhanging the water. I braced myself to make a grab for a branch that was whipping back and forth in the current. As I rushed toward it, I raised my arms and seized it with both hands. I went under but held on, and as the branch stretched to its full length, it tightened and I returned to the surface—just in time to see Ski bearing down on me.

I yelled for him to grab hold of me and stuck my leg out into his path. He caught it and held it tightly. I waited for the branch to break—it held. There the two of us waited, for a strange moment, as Ski pulled on my leg and the raging current pulled at both of us. Slowly, he began to work his way up my leg and body until he could grab the branch where it came out from the tree limb.

I glanced up the creek. To my surprise, there was Bobby, our little mascot, floating down the creek toward us. His Snoopy-like ears were flat out away from his head like large balancing fins, keeping his head level.

I yelled for Ski to grab him as he came by.

As Bobby came abreast of him, Ski reached out, got a handhold in the fur of his neck and tossed him up onto the bank.

Ski inched his way up my leg until he got a good grip on the tree limb and then let go of me. Safely on the bank, he grabbed a large part of the collar of my peacoat and pulled me upward. Sopping wet, cold, and tired, but grateful to be alive, we looked downstream. Lady was nowhere in sight—she had disappeared. Bobby shook the water off his body violently (as dogs always do)—and sat down on his haunches.

We ran, mainly to keep warm, back toward camp, Bobby trotting behind. When we arrived, I headed for the supply tent, and as we entered, Sergeant Hamilton exclaimed, "There's Bobby! I wondered where he went." Fortunately, I was too cold to bother feeling unappreciated.

Bobby went over, flopped down in front of the heater, and promptly fell asleep. We, too, sat down to warm ourselves by the kerosene heater, shivering underneath wool blankets as Ski told Hamilton our story. Quillen threw blankets around us while Hamilton hung our clothes to dry over our new oil heaters.

We put food out every other night that we remained in Camp Pendleton, but there was never any indication that Lady returned.

Fifty-one years later, following the torrential rains of January 10, 1995, Marine Lieutenant Colonel Harry Michael Murdock attempted to find a safe place for his 79 Marines to cross the swollen San Onofre Creek. At almost exactly the same spot that we entered, Murdock was swept downstream and drowned. His body was found the next day, four miles downstream in the delta area of the creek.*

---

*I do not think that was Lady's fate. Before we left camp, Ski reported that he had glimpsed her high on the hill near where a sheepherder grazed his flock of sheep, and that she appeared healthy. She had, it seemed, learned to live without the Marines.

★　★　★

The date for our departure finally came through: February 14, 1944. The orders said that we were to embark from San Diego to a place called "Bravo," although to maintain security they gave no indication where Bravo happened to be. The consensus was that Bravo was Guadalcanal, but there was no way we could be certain. When the supplies arrived—including 125 woolen sweaters and 750 pounds of dry ice-cream mix—we were even less certain.

The supplies also included two thousand cartons of dry dog food, each the size of a one-pound box of table salt. Mixed with water, they were to equal two pounds of moist dog food. I told Hamilton that would last us only a month and to order more.

The colonel's master sergeant came by next day and said that we had to strike all of the tents in our camp and in the Paratroopers' camp. Hamilton figured that there were 270 tents and it would take us four days to do the job. When the tents were struck and hauled away, we would live in one of the mess halls until we boarded our ship.

The men had worked too hard to spend their last days in the States dismantling someone else's tents, so I told the sergeants to have the men fall in and march out of camp every morning as if they are going into the hills to train. Instead they relaxed all day and marched back into camp at quitting time. By regulations, we had to keep half of the men in camp every night. But many did not want their liberty and volunteered to stay in so that the men with wives and girlfriends could go on liberty almost every night until we left.

While the men enjoyed themselves, I spent my last days ensuring that all Marines in the platoons were in perfect condition before we shipped out for Bravo. Peppy, Benny Goldblatt's dog, had suffered a bite on his leg, and before we left, I wanted to make sure that Goldblatt would be able to take proper care of his charge. I told Goldblatt to give Peppy two sulfanilamide tablets every eight hours, but he complained that Peppy was liable to bite him if he stuck his fingers down his throat. "Lieutenant, he ain't the most friendly dog we have, you know." He held out his hands. There were old scars and new red marks indicating recent dog bites. "He bites me all the time," Goldblatt said dejectedly.

I told him that he had to take charge. I took the pill and put my left hand flat on Peppy's top jaw behind his canine teeth, and with my middle two fingers on one side and my thumb on the other, I squeezed gently until Peppy spread his jaws. With the pill between my thumb and index finger of my right hand, I held Peppy's tongue down with my big finger and pushed the pill past his tongue and as far down his throat as I could—then I shut his jaws and held them tight. With one gulp the pill was down.

I told Benny it was his turn. He was to use a command voice, and to keep his actions firm and his movements confident. Goldblatt drew himself up and said in loud voice, "Peppy, Stay." He took Peppy's face in his hand as I had done and pushed the pill into his mouth but was too afraid to ram it down his throat. Peppy promptly spit it out.

I told him to try again—that he must put the pill all the way over the back of Peppy's tongue and then down the throat. I explained that Peppy could not bite him as long as he held his mouth open with his left hand. This time, he shut his eyes, held on tight to Peppy's upper jaw and rammed the pill down Peppy's throat. It stayed down.

"I did it, Lieutenant, I did it," he shouted, amazed at his success.

As he asserted himself more, Peppy would gain confidence in him. Dogs like humans to dominate their relationship. Peppy, like all dogs, really wanted Goldblatt to be in charge; the biting was not an attempt to usurp Goldblatt's authority but to establish some kind of hierarchy where he saw none.

What is true for dog-human relationships is not always true for human-human relationships. After struggling with the Paratroopers and the quartermaster, I had had enough of the hierarchy of the home front Corps and longed for the relaxation of rules that came with war. I was eager to prove the value of the dogs in combat to my superiors and eager, in truth, to prove myself as well. The next day was Valentine's Day. Our present would be a truck that would take men, dogs and supplies to a ship waiting in San Diego.

★ CHAPTER SIX ★

LIFE ABOARD SHIP

The SS *Eugene Skinner* was a Liberty ship, one of hundreds manufactured by wartime industrial wizard Henry Kaiser. By simply welding the metal plates of the sides and frame instead of fastening them with rivets, the production time for building a single ship went from months to a matter of days. In the early days of the war German and Japanese subs had been sinking vessels faster than the Allies could produce them; without Kaiser's innovation, America would not have been able to supply England with the wartime materials needed to stave off Germany until America could fully join the war.

But, when I first saw the *Skinner*, I did not think about our incredible achievements of production, but of my selfish hopes for a first-class ocean voyage—now forever dashed. She rode high in the water of San Diego Harbor listing decidedly to starboard, her sides rusty, and what paint was left on her hull peeling. Sergeant Hamilton assured me that once she had taken on fuel she would straighten right up, but to my eyes the *Skinner* was a sad-looking old scow. I concluded that I would be lucky if I made it to our final destination at all.

The *Skinner* was manned by American merchant marines, the civilians that sailed merchant ships, freighters, tankers, and such. During World War II, thousands of them went down with their ships carrying supplies to our allies and our own armed forces. Our captain, who was Dutch, told Taylor and me that we were bound for

Guadalcanal and our next stop would be New Caledonia. The captain had been in the Atlantic, where the most dangerous convoy work was, and had been sunk four times. This time we would sail alone—the most hazardous way to travel—and so take an indirect route by heading south, almost as far as the Fiji Islands, to avoid Japanese submarines. Due to the *Skinner*'s slowness—her top speed was eight knots an hour—we wouldn't arrive for at least forty days.

To board the *Skinner*, the dogs were removed from their crates, which were hoisted onto the ship and placed in one row on each side of the deck and faced outward. The men were assigned to the *Skinner*'s forward hold, which had originally been designed for freight but had been "remodelled" to provide sleeping quarters for 150 troops. Bunks were stacked four-high along the starboard side, and the galley ran along the port side. Tables and benches occupied the center of the hold where the men could eat, play cards, read, or write letters. The hatch covering the hold had been removed and was replaced with canvas. There was no air-conditioning; instead, the canvas was rolled back on warm nights and sunny days to allow fresh air to enter the hold.

Bill Taylor and I were assigned to the stateroom, topside. I stashed my gear in a corner and took off my field boots, and the moment I put my bare feet on the deck, they burned so badly I hastily retrieved my boots. Although more luxurious than the hold, our stateroom was located directly above the engine room: it was going to be a hot, humid trip.

★ ★ ★

Fifteen minutes into the trip, I got seasick. The ship felt as though it were rolling all over the ocean, but as I went to the head for the fourth time, I glanced out the porthole and saw, to my dismay, that we were still tied to the dock. Except for sick call for the dogs, I didn't emerge from the stateroom for three days. During the first few days, several of the dogs also suffered seasickness. We gave them Donnatal, a mixture of atropine and phenobarbital, but it didn't help them any more than it did me. Dogs and men were left to recover on their own.

We soon settled into a daily routine. Reveille was at 6 A.M, but due to the limited facilities—there were only ten toilets for over 110 men—we were given a full hour to get ready for roll call, held on the afterdeck. The men were dismissed from formation, and during the next hour the dogs were removed from their crates and taken by squads to the fantail, the aptly named poop deck, the raised deck at the rear of the ship. A hose was available to wash down the deck afterward, although solid waste was deposited into GI cans that, along with the garbage from the galley and trash accumulated during the day, were dumped into the sea just before dark. The resulting trail of flotsam would be difficult to follow at night by enemy submarines, and by morning we would be miles away.

At 8 A.M. the men fell back into ranks with their dogs, then peeled off by squads and ran in single file around the deck of the ship several times. Following the morning exercise, the dogs were returned to their crates and the men headed for breakfast. (The dogs were not fed until the afternoon.) Then the men swabbed down the toilet and shower area. They were freed from this task at 10 o'clock and returned to the afterdeck to remove their dogs from the crates and spend time with them.

Lunch was served in two shifts, at 12:30 and 2 P.M., after which the men were required to wash their clothes and clean and oil their weapons to keep them from rusting in the damp, salty sea air. At 4:30 we all gathered on the deck for calisthenics, then the dogs were fed and dinner was served at 6:30. After dinner the men spent their time writing letters home which would be sent at the next port, playing cards, chatting, or reading a paperback book that had been provided by the Red Cross through the ship's library. Lights were out at 10:30.

Every Friday we enlivened the monotony with an inspection of quarters and all personal gear by the officers—meaning Taylor and myself. Uniforms had to be clean, carbines clean and oiled, and the men clean-shaven, with military haircuts. All the while, the *Skinner* slowly slogged on.

The boredom of confinement at sea did have some beneficial side effects. Without encouragement, the men eagerly removed their dogs from their crates and played with them. The men spent hours teaching their dogs tricks, slowly learning every facet of their personalities. Hide-and-seek was a favorite game. At the command Search, the dogs would hunt down socks, belt buckles, K-Bar knives, or anything else hidden on the ship. Objects were concealed in old cardboard boxes stacked on the deck. When the objects were found, the dogs attacked the boxes with their front feet and literally tore them apart. In these unofficial exercises, Pfc. Keith Schaible's Butch was declared the champion. He could find anything that Schaible wanted him to find regardless of where it was hidden or by whom. Butch became so proficient at games that he was later able to locate mines and booby traps buried by the Japanese; he would prove unmatched in his ability to search caves for enemy soldiers or explosives.

The dogs also acquired skills that, frankly, had no military purpose. Some were taught to walk on their hind legs, some on their front with their hind legs stuck up into the air. They learned to shake hands and to catch a piece of pogie bait in midair that had been placed on their noses or flipped upward at a handler's command. Pfc. Bob Johnson taught Spike to lift his leg and on command to urinate on anything—or anyone—next to him. Johnson's secret command was a particular way of twitching the leash that always went undetected by the unsuspecting victim.

Sergeant Barnowsky had come aboard with a new puppy tucked into his jacket. Skeeter, as he came to be known, was a mongrel with a German Shepherd somewhere among his ancestors. Even before he was house-trained, Barney began teaching him basic obedience with one essential difference: Skeeter was trained to do everything backward. For example, when told to sit, Skeeter promptly stood up. Then Barney took the game one step further; when given one command, Skeeter would do the opposite until Barney turned his back. Then Skeeter would assume the correct position—until Barney turned around again. The comedy act grew increasingly intricate as the voyage dragged on. Barney would tell Skeeter to sit up while on a table and Skeeter would go completely limp and slide slowly off the side. When pulled upright, Skeeter would collapse again. While Barney appealed in frustration to the audience, behind his back Skeeter would sit up or do his own tricks. The second that Barney returned his attention to Skeeter, the dog collapsed and Barney would have to catch him to keep him from falling to the deck.

The Barney and Skeeter show was so entertaining that later in the war they were frequently asked to participate in shows for servicemen on the islands and ships of the Pacific. After the war I saw a professional dog trainer on stage in Las Vegas, Nevada, who went through the exact same routine to the delight of his audience. Had he cribbed from World War II's Barney and Skeeter show?

The two dog platoons were not alone aboard the *Skinner*. Along with the merchant marine crew, there was an armed guard from the U.S. Navy commanded by Lieutenant Elvis A. Mooney, a former high-school principal from Bloomfield, Missouri. Mooney was in his mid-thirties, stocky and slightly overweight, with sandy-colored hair that was beginning to thin. Mooney was not by nature an officious man, but thought it integral to the persona of a naval officer that he become a student of naval protocol.

Every morning, dressed in perfectly starched whites, Mooney went on his inspection tour. Along each side of the deck were two batteries of twin 50-millimeter antiaircraft guns, commonly called ack-ack guns, which, at an incredible rate, could throw up a barrage of automatic fire at an enemy aircraft should the situation demand it. Mooney's gunners sat in the chairs on the ack-ack guns or stood at attention beside the 5-inch gun as he walked by. If he found anything awry, he dressed down the offender with awful threats: "If it happens again, I'll nail your left ball to the yardarm." For Mooney, it was always the left ball, and never the right. Of course, it was an idle threat—Mooney never disciplined anybody. When he wasn't visible, the crew mostly basked in the sun.

One morning as Mooney made his tour all dressed out in his whites, he climbed the ladder to the fantail while the dogs were relieving themselves on the deck. Incensed at the desecration of our vessel, he yelled that it was a disgrace and ordered the place cleaned up immediately. He pointed the toe of his white shoe at the closest stool and turned to Pfc. Tex Blalock and screamed, "There's feces all over this deck."

Blalock was an eighteen-year-old from Muleshoe, Texas. He was an intelligent Marine but had little formal education. When Mooney began yelling, Blalock became alarmed. "Feces! Feces!" he shouted. "I don't see no feces, sir!"

Mooney pointed his toe again to a huge dog stool on the deck.

Blalock's face brightened. Recognizing Mooney's mistake and wanting to set him straight, he cried delightedly, "Sir, sir, that ain't feces, that's dog shit!"

Mooney reddened, turned on his heel and left.

★   ★   ★

About ten days after we'd put to sea, we ran into a huge tropical storm. The wind blew spray across the decks, which became awash as huge waves washed over the bow. At times the waves were so high that the bridge, the ship's highest point, seemed like a tiny tree amid mountains of water. The helmsman struggled to keep the ship from broaching as it fought to crest the tops of these cliffs, and the ship shuddered as it plunged through one wave after another, climbing laboriously to the top, plunging down the other side, burrowing its bow in the bottom of the trough, then starting all over again.

We turned the doors of the dogs' crates aft to keep the salt water out and positioned a tarp in front of them as a shield. But the salt water did its damage: two days into the storm, Quillen showed me four dogs that had sore feet. The dogs walked gingerly across the deck, pausing to lick their feet frequently. The flesh between their toes and under their pads was red, inflamed and weeping. I washed the feet with fresh water, dried them and applied iodoform, a drying powder, between the toes and under the footpads. Then I bandaged them and sent the dogs back to their crates.

The following day when the dogs were brought to sick call, I removed the bandaged feet only to find the condition had worsened. The tissue was more inflamed than before and the smell of rotten flesh—the dogs' chewing kept the bandages wet and their tissues infected—filled the air. When the bandages were left off, the dogs persisted in licking their wounds and the salt water continued to irritate the already irritated skin, making the condition worse.

It was Quillen who came up with the solution. As I was cleaning one of the dog's feet, he said he'd be right back. The Corps, it seemed, had sent us off with extra boxes of condoms—thousands of them. At the time the men had joked that the government had more faith in their charms than they had themselves. Quillen had discovered that either there had been a method to the Corps's madness or that we had gotten lucky. If I would bandage each foot and cover it with a "Merry Widow," it would stay dry.

When Quillen returned, we put Duke on the crate that I was using as an examination table, cleaned his infected foot, dried it, powdered it liberally with iodoform, stuffed cotton between the toes and under the pads, rolled several courses of gauze around his paw and enveloped the whole thing in a condom, bound loosely with gauze and tape. I repeated the same treatment with the other dogs that had sore feet.

By the next day the dogs' feet were drier and less inflamed. I continued the regimen, and by the time the sea had calmed several days later, I was able to leave the bandages off. With the absence of salt water soaking their feet and the cessation of their licking, the dogs' paws continued to improve and quickly returned to normal.

There was one other casualty of the rough sea. Pfc. Ed Mullen had fallen and cut all of the tendons in his right wrist on pieces of a China crock he was carrying. In spite of catgut sutures that were suitable for dogs but too large for human tendons, I was able to reattach them, and Mullen regained use of all but his middle finger, which was later repaired at the naval hospital at New Caledonia.

As the ship continued south, the weather growing slowly hotter, we removed the tarp from the front and sides of the dogs' crates, leaving only one over the top to provide shade. We turned the crates outboard, too, in hopes that a breeze might provide more ventilation. The heat in my stateroom had been bad at the beginning of the voyage, but as we progressed southward it became unbearable. I abandoned my torture chamber for the captain's doghouse, a cot covered by a small canvas tent just outside the bridge. The peak of the tent was only two feet above the cot, which allowed just enough space to slide in feet first and head last. The doghouse was meant for the captain to use as a place where he could catch a few winks when the ship was in dangerous water and he needed to be close to the bridge. But in his experience in hostile waters, the time lost in trying to get out of the doghouse and to the bridge would be more than could be spared if a crucial decision was necessary. He told me I was welcome to it. Taylor also abandoned the stateroom, surviving by throwing his mattress out on the deck outside the stateroom at night and back inside in the morning.

One morning, seagulls appeared in the distance on the starboard of the ship. All hands rushed to the deck to watch the birds, knowing that we must be near land. Except for an occasional flying fish—one flew so high that it landed on the deck, thirty feet above waterline—this was the first animal life we had seen since leaving San Diego. The captain told us that the birds were coming from the Fiji Islands a hundred miles away, or possibly from some of the smaller islands south of Fiji. We would arrive in New Caledonia in five days.

That same night, the man on the fantail watch reported a red light on our stern. Hearing the call, I crawled out of the doghouse and went to the bridge. Apparently, the word was passed to the hold because all hands were on deck with their eyes fixed on the blinking red light. The captain searched the area with his field glasses, and declared there was a Japanese submarine off our stern; it must have surfaced to charge its batteries. He had been expecting this since we entered the submarine lanes several days ago, and wondered what had kept the Japanese from appearing for so long.

The sub was about a mile and a half or two miles behind us, but it was hard to tell because it was so dark. As long as the sub stayed that far back, we would be safe, but if it moved closer, we'd have to be ready to defend ourselves.

I was more than a little concerned about this after having watched, only a few days earlier, when Lieutenant Mooney had ordered his gunners to shoot at a crate of garbage that the crew had thrown overboard. All hell broke loose as the 20-millimeter guns had burst into action, the tracer bullets stretching from the muzzles of the guns to the sea around the crate. For five minutes the racket kept up, but when Mooney had called a cease-fire, the crate bobbed along intact: not a single shell had penetrated it. He had then ordered the 5-inch naval gun on the fantail to fire on the target, and the whole ship had shuddered as the gun roared and black smoke rolled out of the muzzle. The shell hit at least a hundred yards short of its target, and a second attempt was so far off that the crate never got splashed.

The captain, perhaps aware of the *Skinner*'s firepower, thought it better not to provoke the vessel, adding that he didn't think it was interested in expending a torpedo on a small ship like the *Skinner*.

For several more days and nights the sub stalked us, perhaps waiting for our ship to join a convoy so that the sub might have more prey. When it finally disappeared, Mooney thought the Japanese commander must have finally seen our 5-inch gun through his periscope and decided he was no match for the *Skinner*. I kept a straight face and my opinions to myself.

As predicted by the captain, on the afternoon of the fifth day, the lookout sounded "Land ho, land ho," and we all rushed onto the

deck to catch our first glimpse of a South Pacific island. Three hours
and thirty minutes later, we steamed into the harbor at Nouméa,
New Caledonia, the late afternoon sun outlining the island in light. I
was pleased to see palm trees and a snowy white beach—it looked
exactly like all of the islands I had seen in movies about the South
Pacific. A local pilot guided us through the channel, and as we got
closer, buildings began to appear. They were not thatched huts; they
were buildings just like those at home: brick, frame and stucco.

After the ship dropped anchor, and as it was getting dark,
Mooney and I clambered aboard a launch and headed for shore. All
of my dreams of the beautiful South Sea islands were soon shattered
by air filled with the aroma of raw sewage. Nouméa was the filthiest
place I had ever seen.

Mooney and I headed for the officers' club, located in the only
large hotel. In the bar of the officers' club a Free French flag was
hung alongside the flags of the United States, Great Britain, Australia
and New Zealand. The British Empire was represented by officers
from New Zealand and Australia, adorned in rakish, wide-brimmed
hats pinned up on one side, and turban-wearing East Indians. There
was even an occasional black officer from the Fiji Scouts, legendary
for their battles against the Japanese in the Solomon Islands. The
six-foot Fiji Scouts were known for creeping up on Japanese outposts, slashing the throats of unsuspecting sentries before their vic-
tims could utter a sound, and crawling silently away. I noticed that
all of them wore long-sheathed knives attached to their Sam Brown
belts even in the club.

All of this was very exciting. Here were men who had fought the
Japanese in the Solomon Islands, and I was desperately hoping to
find out what things were like up there. I sauntered over to listen for
what I hoped would be information I could use when I arrived in

the war zone, but all I got for my snooping were drunken ramblings about the absence of women and tall tales of individual accomplishments. The chatter was the same that took place in gin joints and honky-tonks all over the world, the conversations only slightly more unintelligible because of too much cheap booze.

The next morning I learned that for the seven days that we remained in the harbor at Nouméa, nobody would be able to swim because of lethal sea snakes that populated the waters. Aside from the dogs, the restriction made the biggest difference to Mooney and me, puffy-eyed and lethargic from the previous night of overindulgence. The air was hot and oppressive and there was no breeze flowing over the deck while we were at anchor. The Dobermans were slowly becoming acclimated to the tropical heat, but the longer-haired Shepherds required more time to adjust. To alleviate their suffering, the handlers frequently hosed them down with water in the late afternoon when whatever breeze had been blowing ceased altogether and the heat became stifling.

We had one beautiful sable and white Collie, Tam, who suffered terribly. He panted constantly and even the hosing did not help a great deal. The chief steward loaned me an electric fan, which was kept running on Tam almost continually. It seemed to make him feel better, but after two days he developed a slight cough. Afraid of pneumonia, I reduced the fan's velocity and examined his throat and chest several times a day. The condition did not progress, and I was glad when we put to sea again, this time for Guadalcanal. I cursed the decision of someone back at Lejeune to send him with us, knowing we would be going to the tropics and that Tam would die of exhaustion if sent to race around the jungle at top speed delivering messages. Watching him suffer, I determined that he would be used only for night security, a job he could do effectively without inviting heat stroke. At one point I considered shaving his hair but rejected the idea because there was no shade and the tropical sun beating down on his bare skin would have been excruciating.

We set sail for Bravo, which we now knew to be Guadalcanal, this time, however, in a convoy with other freighters, troopships and an escort of naval fighting ships. As these were hostile waters, we zigzagged our way northward for five days before dropping anchor.

Diminutive Bunkie learned to improve upon his stature by standing up on his hind legs.

The 3rd War Dog Platoon assembled in Camp Lejeune, North Carolina, in 1943, toward the beginning of our training period there. I am in the foreground and Sergeant Ivan Hamilton stands a few paces behind to my left.

Unlike today's military dogs, our dogs were recruited from the civilian population. We did not discriminate by sex. Although dogs admitted into the Marine Corps were *not* supposed to be bred, Bebe would later prove that in spite of safeguards and regulations, nature prevailed and some dogs found a way.

Training. ABOVE: Pal being agitated by a well-padded attacker while his handler, Pfc. Ben Dickerson, looks on. INSET: Dickerson restrains Pal during an attack exercise. Dickerson and Pal—both quiet, serious, and deadly—would make a great team in Guam. BELOW: A patrol exercise at Lejeune. Pfc. Marvin Corff is with Rocky in the left foreground and I am on the far right.

Demolition exercises at Camp Lejeune. By then, dogs that were gun-shy or showed other behavioral traits that made them unsuitable for combat had already been weeded out.

Bobby, our little mascot, helps lead the 3rd War Dog Platoon from Camp Lejeune, North Carolina, to Camp Pendleton, California. From there we would go off to war. I am just in front of Bobby.

Lieutenant William Taylor stands with a captured Japanese war dog. Taylor commanded the 2nd War Dog Platoon, and his platoon and mine worked closely together. A more satisfactory working relationship I have never had, and I am convinced that many dogs and men were saved by our cooperation.

Guadalcanal. ABOVE LEFT: Bill Taylor and I sit with Missy atop one of the crates that were the dogs' homes while at sea. ABOVE RIGHT: I stand with Bobby and Sergeant Ivan Hamilton in front of some of our medical supplies. BELOW: some of our privates first class and war dogs. From left to right: Pfc. Carl Burton with Tam, Pfc's. Dale Quillen and Albert Foster with Fritz, and Pfc's. Thurman Clark and Shirley Duncan with Blitz.

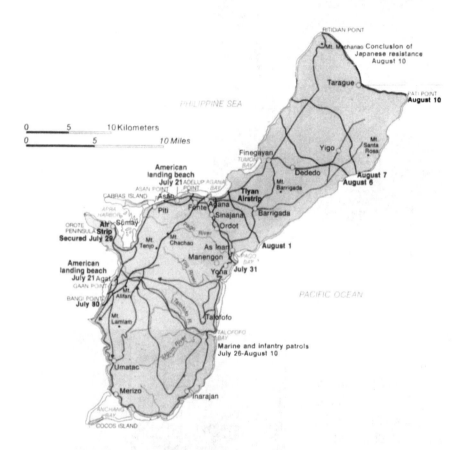

A map of Guam showing key locations and dates. On July 21, 1944, my men and dogs went over the side of our troop transports to help lead the battle for the liberation of Guam, the first liberation of American soil in World War II.

I preside in the "War Dog Sick-Bay" as the chief veterinarian on Guam.

Butch explores an abandoned, war-torn building in Agana, Guam, with Pfc. Keith Schaible and Lieutenant William Taylor. On Guam, as in training, the dogs proved expert at sniffing out even deeply buried mines.

War Dogs Make Japs Miserable.

GUAM ISLAND, July 27.—(Delayed)—(AP)—In the camps of Uncle Sam's battle-hardened devil dogs on Guam Island the leathernecks never tire of praising the faithful American dogs of war that have saved many lives.

The dogs, given into war service by owners, have been of great value in ferreting Jap snipers and uncovering Nippon soldiers hidden in caves. Many have died in the commission of what the marines call heroic deeds.

"Lucky," a Doberman, was sent to the battlefields by his owner, Henry G. Heinrichs of Jackson Heights, Long Island, N. Y.

On Guam Lucky was found crouched close to his wounded handler in a gully near a concrete bridge over Asan River where they had flushed 10 Jap snipers during the night. The bullet-riddled bodies of Nipponese lay under the bridge where they had been wiped out by a marine detail.

He Wouldn't Let Anyone Approach His Dead Master

When the marines started to give first-aid to the wounded handler Lucky growled. But he let them work on his master. When the latter died Lucky moved to the side of the body and would not permit any to approach. Finally Sgt. Vincent Dentino of East Boston, Mass., slipped a noose over the dog's head and pulled him away. The sergeant said, "That's the way these war dogs are—one man dogs."

The provisional war dog company on Guam is commanded by Lt. William Taylor of Union, La.

"Kurt" was a Doberman Pincer owned by Mrs. Bruce W. P. Edgeston of Baltimore. He was up front one dark night with his handler when they spotted a Jap soldier in the brush. The handler tied Kurt to a tree and slipped up on the enemy but was wounded in an exchange of fire.

Dogs Are Credited With Saving Lives of Many Yanks

Marines found the wounded handler and took him back to an aid station. They did not find Kurt, who had been hit by fragments of a mortar shell. Kurt chewed his leash until he was free. He picked up the trail of his handler and raced to the aid station. There he was given blood plasma but he died of a back wound after an operation.

Kurt was one of four war dogs killed during the early fighting on Guam. Another was "Skipper," a Labrador retriever, sent to war by Donnie Philips of Anaconda, Mont. Still another was "Tippy," an Eskimo husky, owned by Victor Lunardini of Chicago.

Two war dogs, "Mitzi," owned by Oliver L. Zeleny of Kyattsville, Md., and "Duchess," owned by James Reece Duncan, Alexandria, Va., became mothers only a few weeks before the Guam invasion. Nevertheless they went ashore with the first assault waves and have made some Jap snipers very unhappy.

A clipping from my hometown paper, the *Farmville Herald* (Farmville, Va.), that relates the positive impact of the war dogs on our overall effort on Guam.

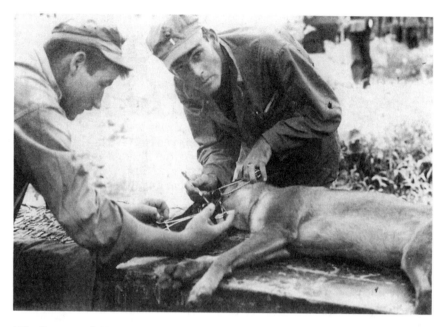

Pfc. Raymond Tomaszewski (left) assists while I operate on a captured Japanese war dog. The Japanese used dogs just as we did, but unlike the men they served, the dogs had the sense not to insist upon the senseless bloodshed of always fighting to the death.

For their success, our dogs, always out in front on dangerous patrols, paid a terrible price for the safety of the men they led. Here, Butch visits the graves of Kurt and Skipper, two of the casualties of the invasion of Guam.

Peppy with his handler, Benton Goldblatt. A bullet fired by a Japanese sniper that pierced Peppy's ear and lodged in his skull had been successfully removed.

ABOVE: Pfc. Marvin Corff poses while handling Rocky in 1945. These dogs were Marines, and as with two-legged Marines, records were kept. Rocky's Dog Record Book shows his enlistment date and serial number. BELOW: a lineup of war dogs in 1945.

An inspection at Camp Lejeune in 1946, after the war. From left to right: General Alfred Noble, Major Harold Gors, Lieutenant Andy Anderson, Lieutenant Colonel L. E. Smith, me (with my tie askew), and Lieutenant Carl Swope. When I returned to Camp Lejeune in April 1945, I found, to my horror and disgust, that some of the dogs that had served with us in battle had already been destroyed.

HCG/jkg

WAR DOG TRAINING SCHOOL
SCHOOLS REGIMENT, MARINE TRAINING COMMAND
CAMP LEJEUNE, NORTH CAROLINA.

27 August 1945

SCHOOL MEMORANDUM)
: WAR DOG DETRAINING AND SEPARATION.
NUMBER 4 - 1945)

References: (a) Marine Corps Dispatch No. 182134.
               (b) MTC GenO No. 13-45, dated 24Aug45.

1.   In accordance with reference (a) and (b) the War Dog Training
School will suspend from all further Combat Training for students and dogs.

2.   Effective Monday 27 August 1945, the War Dog Training School will
initiate a detraining program for all Marine War Dogs so that they may be suitable
for return to civilian life.

3.   The War Dogs will be kenneled under the present strength into
four (4) Kennel Groups and each dog not in the dog hospital will receive the training and care as set forth in the new training schedule.

4.   Dog Handlers will be shifted from one (1) Group to another in
order that the dogs will become familiar with several persons and instil confidence
and mutual respect between man and dog; enabling the dog to again become rehabilitated for return to normal civilian life.

5.   The dogs on the roster of the school will be segregated into the
four (4) Kennel Groups according to their various temperamental attributes or
amount of training they have received. Dogs who have an unsuitable temperament or
who have received advanced agitation training will receive additional attention of
the handlers under the supervision and direction of the dog trainers and his assistants.

6.   When dogs are considered to be temperamentally and physically
rehabilitated for return to civilian life, the Head Trainer and Veterinarian will
submit a joint report on the temperamental and physical condition of each dog to
the Commanding Officer in writing, with recommendations for final disposition, for
transmittal to higher authority.

7.   Dogs possessing temperaments which are incorrigibly vicious, or
one that cannot be fully rehabilitated with complete trust for return to civilian
life after a fair course of detraining, will be so reported in writing to the
Commanding Officer. State the disqualifying conditions either temperamental or
physical, with recommendations for final disposition, for transmittal to higher
authority.

8.   The War Dog Training School thus now becomes a detraining and
separation unit for all Marine War Dogs. All personnel will divert their energy
and experience to a successful detraining and rehabilitation program so that the
Marine War Dogs of World War II will continue to be regarded with the sincere high
respect and admiration for their valorous and heroic deeds which they have contributed to the defeat of the enemy of the United Nations.

HAROLD C. GORS
Major, USMCR,
Commanding.

The original memorandum, issued by Commanding Officer Major
Harold C. Gors, that established the war dog detraining program, one of
the most important documents in the long history of the dogs in the U.S.
military. It is incontrovertible proof that military dogs can be and have
been successfully returned to civilian life.

The original War Dog Cemetery at Asan, Guam. It was destroyed by a typhoon in 1963 and moved to the jungle in the township of Dededo. When I returned to Guam in 1989 to visit it, I was shocked to see the little grave markers toppled over and the grounds in a state of total neglect.

The present-day War Dog Cemetery at the U.S. Naval Base at Orote Point, Guam. Veterans and supporters of the war dogs, myself included, fought hard so that the dogs we served with could have this, a final resting place worthy of their sacrifice. It was dedicated on July 21, 1994.

25 MARINE WAR DOGS GAVE THEIR LIVES LIBERATING
GUAM IN 1944. THEY SERVED AS SENTRIES, MESSENGERS, SCOUTS,
THEY EXPLORED CAVES, DETECTED MINES AND BOOBY TRAPS.

SEMPER FIDELIS

KURT	YONNIE	KOKO	BUNKIE
SKIPPER	PONCHO	TUBBY	HOBO
NIG	PRINCE	FRITZ	EMMY
MISSY	CAPPY	DUKE	MAX
BLITZ	ARNO	SILVER	BROCKIE
BURSCH	PEPPER	LUDWIG	RICKEY

TAM (BURIED AT SEA OFF ASAN POINT)

GIVEN IN THEIR MEMORY AND ON BEHALF OF THE SURVIVING MEN
OF THE 2nd AND 3rd MARINE WAR DOG PLATOONS, MANY OF WHOM
OWE THEIR LIVES TO THE BRAVERY AND SACRIFICE OF THESE
GALLANT ANIMALS

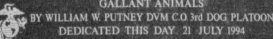 BY WILLIAM W. PUTNEY DVM C.O. 3rd DOG PLATOON
DEDICATED THIS DAY 21 JULY 1994

CHAPTER SEVEN

GUADALCANAL

We arrived at Lunga Point, Guadalcanal, at 11 A.M., fifty-seven days after departing San Diego. We bid goodbye to our friends on the *Skinner,* the men giving our ship's excellent mess sergeant a rousing cheer. I shook hands with the captain and thanked him for a safe and friendly voyage. Landing craft came alongside, took us ashore and dumped us unceremoniously among a grove of coconut palms to await land transportation. Our gear, crates and supplies were brought in and summarily piled on the beach.

Other than some Quonset huts and a few thatched huts, there was not much there other than several freighters, tied to the dock and unloading cargo. Guadalcanal is situated in the Solomon Islands north of Australia and southeast of New Guinea. It was a British possession that had been captured by the Japanese early in 1942 and was used as a jumping-off place for the invasion of Australia. Most of Australia's men were fighting in the African desert against Rommel's Afrika Korps, and the country was virtually defenseless. The 1st Marine Division landed on Guadalcanal in the fall of 1942 and successfully wrested the island from the Japanese. This was a great turning point in the battle for the Pacific, and the first defeat of the Japanese in World War II. Now Guadalcanal was being used as a staging area for the beginning of the arduous march toward Japan itself.

The air on the island was close and hot. We were now back north almost to the Equator; a handful of coconut palms afforded us much-needed shade. In spite of it, the dogs were panting and their tongues hung out. Sergeant Hamilton warned us not to drink the milk from the coconuts lying around on the ground because we could contract diarrhea. Eating their meat, however, would be okay.

Taking him at his word, Pfc. Bruce Wellington, who handled a German Shepherd messenger dog named Little Prince, clambered up a coconut tree and tossed down unripe, green coconuts. The men cut off the ends with their K-Bar knives and dumped the milk into their canteen cups for the dogs. When the dogs had satisfied their thirst, the men drank from the same canteen cups.

Bob Johnson picked up a coconut from the ground and began to rip off the husk. Spike, his red Doberman, got into the act, and Johnson showed him how to husk the coconut with his paws by ripping the husks apart with his hands. Spike attacked the coconut, ripping at the stringy fibrous husk with his teeth and paws, and tore it off completely in about two minutes. Not to be outdone, other handlers got their dogs into the act and soon all the dogs were growling, biting and tearing husks off coconuts. Once husked, the coconuts were broken open, and the meat was extracted with K-Bar knives and eaten by the men and dogs. Hamilton opined that we could go into the copra business: the dogs could husk coconuts faster than the natives.

Our camp, twenty miles down the island, was called The Coconut Grove and was already home to the 3rd Marine Division. Our tents were pitched for us about a mile and a half down the road from the rest of the division, surrounding a large mess tent fully equipped with a field kitchen but with no personnel in sight. In addition to the mess tent, there was a large storage tent for our supplies and a smaller one for the dog sick bay. The crates were laid out in a grove of mahogany trees and the dogs were secured to their stakes and chains, rusty from the salt water during the long voyage.

The tents on Guadalcanal were pitched differently from else-where. About five feet out from each corner, a six-foot bamboo stake, three inches in diameter, had been sunk into the ground. To keep it from being pulled back toward the tent, a guy rope in line with the center pole was attached to the top of the stake and stretched to a tent peg in the ground several feet outward. Between the stakes on each corner was strung a bamboo pole. Instead of hanging down to the ground, the side flaps of the tent were stretched outward and tied to the bamboo stringers. The suspended sides in-creased the usable space of the tent, but the principle advantage was that air could pass through the tent, providing a slight breeze and rendering the temperature just barely bearable. By the time we were all squared away, it was almost midnight, but no cooks showed up, so the men and the dogs ate C rations from our stores.

On the first morning of our stay on the Canal, the banging of pots and pans awakened us. When I got to the galley tent, a tall, slen-der sergeant was working over the stove. He introduced himself and said he had been sent down from the Reconnaissance Company. He and his mess crew would provide us with chow as long as we were attached to the Recon Company, but he was to continue to report to the CO of the Recon Company.

The breakfast was not spectacular. For the first time of what would be many times, I experienced powdered eggs, in this case overcooked and tasting strongly of sulfur. The mess sergeant's feeble attempt at hotcakes also didn't go over too well, and the men made no attempt to hide their disgust. Nothing is more important to the Marine at the business of war than his mess—the men looked at Taylor and me as if they had been betrayed.

Inquiries about our relationship to the Reconnaissance Company went to no avail. We were attached to Recon for administrative purposes and were to report to the CO of the Recon Company for endorsement of all our orders. While the enlisted men suffered at the mess sergeant's inexperienced hands, Taylor and I were to take our mess with the officers of the 25th Construction Battalion. (It was not practical for an outfit as small as ours to have its own officers' mess and the Seabees were located just across the creek from our camp. Walt Disney had designed their logo, a bee flying at sea appropriate to the abbreviation "CBs.") At fifteen minutes before noon, Taylor and I forded a small creek and arrived at our neighbors' mess hall, a screen-sided building with a sheet-metal roof. The officer in charge of the mess met and welcomed us. He asked for our date of rank and, seeing the puzzled look on our faces, explained that Navy officers were assigned seats according to their seniority— the more senior officers sitting, in order, toward the front. We were never, under any circumstances, to move up the table even if a seat was empty. All officers were to wait until the commanding officer had taken his seat before seating themselves; nor could any officer leave the table before the CO rose. If we wanted to leave for any reason, we were to stand and ask permission of the CO before leaving the table. (He cautioned us under his breath not to use frivolous excuses to leave the mess and not to make a habit of it.) When the CO appeared, we were to approach him and introduce ourselves. He would acknowledge our introduction and invite us to join his mess.

We were introduced to a warrant officer by the name of McKirgen, a loading officer whose seat was one below mine. The officers filed into the mess hall and took their places at their assigned seats, McKirgen steering us gently toward ours. The CO, a full commander, entered the mess and took his place at the head of the table. The mess officer nodded to us and we approached the CO and introduced ourselves to him.

"Gentlemen," said the CO, "may I introduce Marine Lieutenants William Taylor and William Putney of the Marine War Dog Platoons just across the creek. They will be taking mess with us. Please welcome them."

"Here, here," said the officers in unison.

"Be seated," said the CO.

We took our places. Taylor whispered to me that this was like something out of *Gunga Din*.

I told him to shut up and eat. If we got thrown out of there, we would be back eating burned powdered eggs with the men. Besides, combat would soon do away with such niceties.

★   ★   ★

The following day, General Allen Turnage, commanding the 3rd Marine Division, issued an order to begin the field exercises that would help to ready us for combat. Upon receiving his directive, Taylor and I set about determining the deployment of our troops. We divided the two platoons into two sections, one made up of scout dogs and handlers and the other of messenger dogs and handlers. The assignment would be for each regiment, six handlers and their six scout dogs and twelve handlers and their six messenger dogs, respectively. The units would be under the command of Bill Taylor with the 9th Marine Regiment; Raymond Barnowsky, the 21st Marine Regiment; and Sergeant Al Edwards, the 3rd Marine Regiment. Edwards was a tall, slender twenty-three-year-old from North Carolina. In typical Marine fashion he was dubbed "Bones." I was to command the remaining men and dogs and, along with the war dog hospital, be with division headquarters. We sent this plan with the names of the men to the division personnel officer, Major Bob Kriendler, and it was approved as submitted.

Once in combat, the assignment of our troops would be the same, so it was essential that these units learn to function efficiently as soon as possible. Rumor had it that the division was in the training stage for an upcoming invasion; we were going to invade Truk in the Caroline Islands. Truk was the most heavily defended island in the South Pacific, and nobody wanted anything to do with it. In the end, the scuttlebutt was wrong. In due time we learned that we would invade and liberate the island of Guam, in the Mariana Islands, a possession of the United States that was captured in the early days of the war by the Japanese in their drive toward Australia.

At a meeting of all officers of units of battalion size and up, plus all commanding officers of supporting units, we were given a plan of attack for the selected island we were to capture. Maps of the island were distributed, stripped of place-names, but there were enough older officers and enlisted men that had served on Guam to recognize it. The secret was soon out and we were cautioned not to even mention the word Guam for fear that the Japanese would somehow discover our intentions and increase their defensive fortifications.

We met the regimental commanders, Colonel Craig of the 9th Marines, Colonel Hall of the 3rd Marines, and Colonel Hogaboom of the 21st Marines. When the exercises for the 21st and 3rd Marines were published, Taylor went with Barnowsky to introduce him to the operations officer of the 21st and I went to the 3rd with Sergeant Edwards. Both were well received, and we told the operations officers that, from now on, the sergeants would be in charge of the war dog units attached to the respective regiments during training and also for landing and support during the coming campaign.

We were given daily schedules of maneuvers of the regiments, and we marched from our camp down the main roadway as we went to our assignments. Whenever the dog units came marching along the road, Marines came bounding out of their tents to see the dogs go by, entranced by the idea of our dogs going off to war. It was a cheering contrast to the abuse the men had taken from the Raiders at Camp Pendleton. These men, veterans of the treacherous fighting of Bougainville, were aware of the contributions of the dogs of the 1st War Dog Platoon there.

★ ★ ★

Nothing ever went completely right on the Canal. Bugs were a constant problem. Regulations called for all personnel to stuff their pants legs into their socks after sundown to help protect against mosquito bites, and anyone caught with his pants outside his socks was severely reprimanded. Guadalcanal had a deadly kind of malignant malaria spread by mosquitoes. Nearly all of the Marines of the 1st Division that made the original invasion of Guadalcanal contracted it. Keeping pants tucked into socks, taking Atabrine tablets at mealtime, and spraying the island with DDT were all measures taken to help prevent the troops from getting infected. (Dogs, fortunately, are not susceptible to the disease.)

But many of the problems on the Canal were the Marines' own doing. There were not enough stevedores from the service command to unload all of the ships bringing supplies to the island, so men from combat units were ordered to go to Lunga Point for stevedore duty. One squad of our men under Sergeant Dentino was sent to Lunga Point when our turn came. I was surprised when the men volunteered for a duty that was despised by all the other troops on the island. The heat in the holds of the ships was almost unbearable and the humidity oppressive—stevedore duty was backbreaking, thankless work.

The following afternoon, when Taylor and I returned from the field, we discovered why. All hands were sitting around drawing on cigars—it smelled like the camp was on fire. The unloading detail had returned with boxes and boxes of cigars, and they were generous with their largesse: I was offered one box that contained two hundred fine Havana cigars. It had been addressed to an admiral. My god, I thought, some kind soul had sent a box of cigars to an admiral and it had gotten rerouted to the war dog platoons. I glanced at Taylor, hands out and palms up.

He motioned me outside and said that we had better leave it alone. If we were to try to get the cigars back on track to the admiral, we could get court-martialed. We agreed: we had never seen any cigars.

The men were enterprising with their stevedores' bounty. By trading (stolen) goods they convinced a pair of Seabees carpenters to make them some "authentic war clubs" out of mahogany from trees on the island, which they then traded to the crews of ships for eggs, fresh meat, occasionally fresh vegetables, fruits and booze. The alcohol, sadly, they had to hide from Taylor and me. If they were caught with it, punishment was severe, and they did not want to put their COs in an impossible position. Soon these former innocents were the best thieves on Guadalcanal. After a month on stevedore duty they could case a ship from topside to the lowest hold in less than a half-hour.

Up at Lunga Point was an ordnance depot that among other things had a stockpile of wrecked and worn-out vehicles of all kinds. (There was always a shortage of jeeps, recons, trucks and even airplanes in the Marine Corps, though the Army seemed to have all they needed.) Ordnance allowed personnel stationed on the island to come to the yard and if possible piece together enough parts to make a vehicle in running condition, and because the vehicles were salvage, no accounting was made. If an outfit shipped out, the vehicle was abandoned or given to some other unit for a small fee.

In his book *Tales of the South Pacific,* James Michener tells of a torpedo bomber pieced together with hay-baling wire and used to carry loads of whiskey on milk runs from Australia for the thirsty warriors of Guadalcanal. When radio contact was made with the overloaded beast coming up the slot in territory patrolled by the Japanese, fighters from Henderson Field on Guadalcanal flew out to escort it and its priceless valuable cargo home.

Our men did not manage quite so well, but it was not for lack of trying. They succeeded in repairing a half-track from Ordnance and drove it back to the dog camp. It was a horrible-looking machine: it had no 75-millimeter gun or machine-gun mounted on it; the metal sides of the rear body were dented in; and the Marine Corps green paint, even though covered with mud, looked like it had been painted on by hand. There was a hole in the front armor where a bazooka or some antitank missile had penetrated it. Even the lettering looked amateurish. But the engine purred just like it was new, and the men made wonderful use of their latest acquisition.

Then, a few days into our enjoyment of the half-track, an Army lieutenant colonel came to us and said that he was missing a vehicle that had been recently unloaded. He had heard that the dog outfit had a half-track and wondered, putting the accusation mildly, if by chance it was his half-track. I said yes, we did have one, but it could not be his: the men had pieced it together up at Ordnance themselves. It was sadly damaged, and we used it only to haul water and, I confessed, for recreation.

The Army colonel examined the half-track, recently returned from a pleasant afternoon ride with Ski, Missy and two Dobermans. He was sorry, he concluded, that he had bothered me. His half-track had been brand-new—this dilapidated machine was definitely not his. When he had left, I saw Ski standing off to one side with a grin. Why, I asked, was he smiling?

Because, the Army colonel never looked for the serial number on the half-track, he said.

The track, it turned out, wasn't salvage at all. The Army had unloaded about a hundred half-tracks and parked them next to the dock our stevedores were working on. They didn't need them for fighting on the Canal anymore, our guys reasoned, so one Marine just got in a half-track, started it up, and drove off. No one stopped him, so he kept going until he reached our camp.

A new half-track would have stuck out like a sore thumb, so the men shot a hole in it with a bazooka they had scrounged, threw hand grenades against its sides, painted it Marine Corps green, and threw mud on it. It looked like it had gone through the battle of Tenarue Ridge, but come to think of it, the engine sounded like it had just come out of the Chrysler plant.

I told Taylor about it, and as in other touchy situations his logical mind immediately offered the simplest and best possible solution. Because the vehicle wasn't destined for combat, we were not depriving soldiers of it who would have otherwise put it to good use. Either we would enjoy it or some other grunts would—

it might as well be us. When we left, we would just leave it here and the Army would get it back anyway. They would only be without it for a matter of weeks.

I agreed, but felt that the looting of ships had to be put to an end. The pickings had become very slim and the men began to steal boxes even though they had no idea what the boxes contained. I came across four boxes in camp, broken wide open, which contained nothing but airplane parts. As long as they stole things from the Army and the Navy that they could use to make their life better on this miserable island, I told the men once I had assembled them, I looked the other way. But if the airplanes at Henderson Field (the Canal's lone airstrip) couldn't fly because a bunch of knuckleheads in the dog platoons didn't have anything else left to steal, it was a detriment to the war effort. I told them to box the parts up on the double. From now on they would only go on an unloading detail when their turn came and then with Sergeants Barnowski or Hamilton.

I had put a stop to the thieving, but I didn't blame the men for what they had done. Using the quirks of the Marine Corps for personal advantage was the only way to survive out of combat duty—and the Corps was constantly providing us with oddities that could be made to work in our favor. I mentioned to one of the Seabees officers that we had been outfitted with some strange things indeed for troops headed for Guam: the hundreds of sweaters and 750 pounds. of ice cream. The minute I mentioned dry ice-cream mix, all eyes lit up: Did we really have 750 pounds of dry ice-cream mix?

I laughed. It was true. But instead of laughing with me at such a ridiculous thing as issuing ice-cream mix to a dog outfit, the Seabees stared at me with serious expressions on their faces. A lieutenant offered us five gallons of ice cream for our troops every Sunday for lunch in return for the ice-cream mix.

I didn't wait for a consultation with Taylor; the ice-cream mix was theirs.

A truck would be over to our camp this afternoon to pick up the mix, and it would take another a week or so to scrounge enough compressors and tubing to put together the machinery to make the ice cream itself. But by that Sunday, we would have five gallons of ice cream. Sure enough, the Seabees retrieved a few junk compressors that had previously powered air tools from the scrap pile and founded what was to become the "Guadalcanal Ice Cream Factory."

The ice cream that came out of the factory was as good as any in the world. How good does ice cream taste in a place where day after day the temperature exceeds a hundred degrees in the shade; where the humidity is always overly high; where ice is not available in any form and the water one drinks is warm and musty-tasting from the sides of the canvas Lister bags in which it is stored? I can no longer remember, exactly. But I can remember savoring every lick, and I know that in the many years that have elapsed since, no meal, however great, nor ice cream, however sweet, has surpassed it.

★　★　★

Between stolen cigars and ice cream, the men were managing well, but, after we had been on Guadalcanal for about a month, some of the dogs began to get sick. Adjusting to the tropical downpours was difficult for them; their crates never thoroughly dried out and the kennel area was constantly mired in mud. Some began to cough. I checked them several times a day for a few days, and nothing serious developed except in one dog, Scout, who did not improve and came down with pneumonia. He responded slowly to intravenous feedings and sulfa drugs and fortunately made a full recovery in two weeks.

But a far more devastating illness would soon present itself, one that threatened to wipe out all of our dogs. I first got wind of it when Ski reported that Adamski's Big Boy had grown weak in the hindquarters. Adamski was a neat-looking Polish kid from Chicago. He had been an amateur boxer and a very good one and regularly boxed at the matches held in camp every Saturday night. Big Boy was not so dapper: his ears were not cropped, and his bones seemed to poke through his skin. But his mind made up for his lack of physical attractiveness.

I examined the dog carefully but could find no reason for the weakness; he had no temperature, no indication of infection, and no sign of having been wounded. Yet within several days his condition had worsened to such an extent that he wobbled like a drunken sailor when he walked. A day or so later he had developed complete posterior paralysis; now he walked only by dragging his hind legs. He responded to needle pricks along his spine, but had sensitivity only in the vicinity of the prick. Even pain did not cause him to draw up his legs as he should have.

Worried and thoroughly stumped, I turned to Dr. Van dar Veer, the medical officer of the Seabees, for help. A full commander in the Navy Medical Corps, he had taught medicine at one of the prestigious midwestern medical schools in civilian life. Dr. Van dar Veer suggested I do a spinal tap on Big Boy and send the spinal fluid to the division laboratory for examination. Back at the war dog hospital I shaved the lumbar area of Big Boy's back over the spinal column, scrubbed it with tincture of green soap, painted it with iodine to keep the samples safe from contamination, inserted a needle into the spinal cavity, and withdrew a milliliter of spinal fluid and took it to the lab. It would be two weeks before I could expect an answer.

In the meantime, Pfc. Charlie Jones's dog Monty began to present the same symptoms. First he wobbled; then the condition worsened until he was completely down in the hindquarters. He was followed by Bob Johnson's Spike and Bruce Wellington's Little Prince, the only Shepherd affected. Both dogs deteriorated rapidly and were soon completely paralyzed in their hind legs.

Fear and depression demoralized the two platoons. The men whose dogs remained healthy were terrified that their dogs would succumb any day to the mysterious paralysis. The men whose dogs were afflicted remained with their animals day and night. To keep the dogs from dragging their hind legs in the mud, the men lifted them by their waists and helped them walk on their front feet. The expressions on their faces as they looked at me for help was devastating. I felt helpless; I could offer no assurances.

Taylor thought it was a matter of time until all the dogs came down with it. Could it be, he asked, that some infection was spreading from one dog to the next? I shrugged and told Taylor that my examinations had revealed nothing so far: no temperature, no vomiting, no diarrhea, no respiratory symptoms—nothing but paralysis. I began to fear, like Taylor, that there was some unknown virus at work and became increasingly certain that it would spread to all the dogs.

I caught up with Dr. Van dar Veer after lunch at the officers' mess and told him about my frustration. In spite of my training, I was absolutely helpless, as if I knew nothing. He could offer no advice other than to trust my instincts. Go back to my dogs, he said, and go over their living conditions. Think about all the things that had changed since I got to the island. Write them all down and then think again. The dogs were not sick before, now they were all getting sick. There had to be a difference in environment: What was it?

At Dr. Van dar Veer's prodding, I stopped feeling sorry for myself and went back to work. I listed all the physical conditions that the dogs lived under on the island and, one by one, discarded them all as unable to cause the symptoms that were devastating the dogs. I wrote down all the working conditions of the dogs, but nothing seemed to be capable of effecting the change I had documented. Then I began to think about the dogs' diet. We were still feeding them the dry dog food we had brought with us from the States, and sometimes we added portions of the men's C rations to the dry food to make it more palatable and to supply additional protein. There was no logical reason why rations designed for humans should cause any serious medical condition in dogs, particularly since our C rations were only a supplement to the dogs' regular, specially formulated diet.

Some of the men, however, had supplemented the C rations and dry dog food with frozen carp from New Zealand since we had arrived in Guadalcanal. (A supply depot at Lunga Point offered it as a source of raw meat.) The dogs loved it and jumped into the air to catch a piece of fish on the fly. I vaguely remembered reading about a condition that developed on a fox farm in Minnesota where foxes that were fed frozen carp from the Great Lakes developed posterior paralysis. It was later determined that the fish contained an anti–vitamin B-1. An antivitamin is a substance that can prevent the absorption of vitamins into the bloodstream or, worse still, destroy a vitamin once it has been ingested. The body soon develops a vitamin deficiency and, among other things, vitamin B-1 deficiency can cause posterior paralysis by stunting communication along the nerves that transmit motor stimuli from the brain to the muscles of the rear legs.

I immediately put the dogs on a diet of C rations and dry dog food only and ordered a supply of injectable vitamin B-1. I pumped it into the veins of the afflicted dogs, praying as the vitamin ran into their blood system that it would help. I consulted Dr. Van dar Veer, too, who told me the disease was called Chastek paralysis. It had been discovered by a veterinarian at the University of Minnesota and named after the owner of the fox farm I had read about. It was similar to the "locomotor ataxia" suffered by some alcoholics who didn't get enough B-1 and over a long period of time developed ataxia of the legs so severe that they shuffled when they walked. Keep going with the treatment, he urged. If I was correct, the dogs had not been effected long enough to be permanently damaged.

Before the lab report on the spinal fluid came back, the dogs began to improve. The lab findings, as I'd suspected, were negative, and the dogs responded to the B-1. Little Prince recovered after his third injection; Big Boy, who had come down with it first, was the last to recover, in about three weeks' time.

An injured two-legged Marine made his final, full recovery as well. The next day Ed Mullen returned from the New Caledonia Hospital, his middle finger now working fine. I asked him what the Navy doctor that had repaired his tendons had said about my surgery, hoping to get some great accolades. He said that when the doctor had opened his wrist, he exclaimed, "What did that guy sew you up with? Rope?" as he pulled out strand after strand of the catgut.

★   ★   ★

Maneuvers with the regiments were drawing to a close and the Battle of Guam drawing near. There would be one final maneuver that involved the entire division and its support groups and would serve as a dry run for our landing on Guam.

All of our transports and landing craft gathered off the beach down the road from the Coconut Grove while we walked the five miles to the beach and waited on the sand for the landing craft to pick us up and deliver us to our transport. As planned, Taylor and his men and dogs were on a ship anchored at Lunga Point. Barnowsky with the 21st Marines, Edwards the 3rd Marines, and I, along with the sick bay and the division headquarters unit, were assigned to the same ship, the USS *Aquarius.*

Mac McKirgen, from the Seabees, was the loading officer on the ship and would share the staff room with me. McKirgen explained that we would be cruising down the coast all night and would arrive at Tassaforanga at daylight, where we were to land with the dogs, move inland to our assigned units and then come back to the ship to return to Coconut Grove.

For this trip men and dogs would crap out on the after deck. On the real trip to Guam we would stack the dog crates on the afterdeck and the men would be quartered below. I went out on deck to see that the men were settled in. Barnowsky met me before I got to the afterdeck and said he had heard that the men were to put their blankets down and sleep on the deck with their dogs.

I told him I was afraid this was so, but when we returned to the ship to go to Guam, the crates would be on the afterdeck, the same as when they were on the *Skinner,* and the men would be assigned quarters. Tassaforanga was fortunately part of the Canal, and not far away. We would put to sea tonight and land there in the morning.

Tassaforanga had been was one of the last parts of Guadalcanal to be held by the Japanese, and they had used it to deliver supplies and reinforce the island until their final retreat. Our torpedo boats and destroyers sank many of the barges off Tassaforanga, some laden with thousands of Japanese soldiers. When the last barge had left Tassaforanga, the battle for Guadalcanal was over.

The ship headed to sea at dusk, and before time for evening chow, my old malady had struck. I was bent over the john heaving when Mac came in. "I know this is not the time to ask, but are you going to chow?" he chuckled.

"I don't think so, Mac. You go ahead, I'll just die here."

I was sick all night and was still sick when general quarters was sounded the next morning and we were directed to take our positions for landing. I hurried down to the deck and joined my troops where the sergeants had gathered them with packs on their backs and dogs in their harnesses waiting to go over the side. The cargo net had been lowered and the landing craft were circling in the water.

I heard a voice on the loudspeaker: "Dog platoons, stand by to enter landing craft." One of the landing craft approached the side of the ship below the landing net and stopped. "Land the dog platoons," the loudspeaker commanded.

Barney's men moved to the side of the railing, and Billy Baldwin went over the side and into the boat. Ben Dickerson put the long leash on Pal and lowered him over the side. As Baldwin reached up for Pal, the boat sank into a canyon between swells leaving Pal dangling in the air. I yelled to Ben to drop the leash when he felt Pal hit the deck. When the boat rose in the water on the following wave, Pal hit the deck and Dickerson dropped the leash. The first dog was safely aboard the landing craft. In spite of moving as fast as safely possible, it took more than an hour to lower the sixty dogs. As we headed to the beach, we passed a rusting Japanese freighter that had sunk and several barges, their wheelhouses barely visible above the waves that crashed over them.

My nausea lasted until the landing craft slid up the beach and lowered its ramp. I was the first out and the men followed. I asked the first MP that I saw on the beach how to get to division head-quarters. He pointed straight ahead and we charged inland. My sea-sickness had disappeared and within several hundred yards, I saw our commander, Lieutenant Colonel Newton Barkley, CO Head-quarters Battalion, who told me to have my men fall out and wait for further orders. After an hour we returned to the ship.

There I discussed the length of time it took to get the dogs off the ship and into the landing craft. McKirgen, a veteran of the Bougainville landing, said we would not have that much time to spare when landing on Guam: the ship was going to be loaded with ammunition, artillery shells and explosives. Our cargo had to get to the beach quickly, or lives would be lost. I told him I never expected it to take an hour or more to get our dogs off the ship, and we agreed it was intolerable. When we practiced on the mock-up at Lejeune, the earth didn't bob up and down like the sea; the bottom man could pull the dog as far away as was needed to keep the dog from getting tangled in the net. The real thing, I worried, would be more difficult still.

We had only four days ashore before embarking for Guam. During that time, the freighters, oilers and PA (primary troop) ships were loaded with everything except the troops. Destroyers, PC boats (the small craft that would patrol the perimeter of the convoy) and larger vessels including cruisers, aircraft carriers and battleships gathered offshore ready to escort the convoy to the Mariana Islands.

The Seabees threw a final party, lasting until 1 A.M., in the officers' mess. All the allotment of whisky from the Officers' Club was drawn and put on the table and a dinner of fresh salad—where the fresh lettuce and tomatoes came from, I have no clue—vegetables and T-bone steaks cooked to order were the highlights of the evening. For dessert, we had the last of the ice cream from the now famous Guadalcanal Ice Cream Factory. Taylor and I stumbled back to camp to find that the men, too, had thrown their own party, with liquor they had brewed in a hidden (illegal) still.

The few men still able to stand after a night of the foul home brew were singing at the tops of their lungs, and others were passed out on the ground. When the singers saw us arrive, they stopped their serenading, gathered their drunken comrades from the ground and sheepishly staggered to their tents. Our last night on Guadalcanal had come to an end.

The next day the men looked more like they were coming from a battle than going to one. After breakfast, they gathered all of their belongings and put them in their packs. What they could not carry, they crammed into their dog's crate. The whole procedure was carried out agonizingly, in slow motion. The column dragged itself out of camp for the last time, me pushing them from the rear as Sergeant Edwards pulled them from the front. Every time someone slid back toward me, I threatened him, and torrents of boozy-smelling sweat poured from the men as they plodded along the road on the long march to the beach. We were ten minutes late, but the landing craft were even later.

When the column was halted, all hands dropped to the ground, breathing hard in an effort to catch their breath. The dogs lay down panting.

It was a still, hot day, and out to sea I could see the approaching landing crafts moving slowly across the horizon, their silhouettes distorted by the glare of the morning sun off the water. Finally, they arrived and we loaded our gear and headed for the ship. Mac McKirgen was laughing from the rail at our appearance as we approached.

Our ship was the USS *Aquarius*. It was one of the ships designed to carry troops, and this particular one was a U.S. Coast Guard ship.

Around the entire ship landing craft hung from halyards. The men would have good quarters, separate from the crew's. The afterdeck, much larger than the *Skinner*'s, allowed more room for the dogs to exercise. This time we would not travel alone but would be part of a convoy made up of warships of the Seventh Fleet and the transports carrying troops of the 3rd Amphibious Corps. Destroyers were in front, cruisers and battleships in the center, and aircraft carriers and troop ships in the rear. With all of the ships anchored together in the Canal's small lagoon, they looked like sampans crowding the harbor of Hong Kong. The dogs seemed to be pleased with their new, temporary home; I, too, was glad to put Guadalcanal behind me.

CHAPTER EIGHT

LANDING

We went to Guam by way of Kwajalein, a part of the Marshall Islands. It is an atoll in the west central Pacific Ocean, consisting of a group of islets surrounding a large lagoon. The atoll had been heavily fortified by the Japanese and was taken by the Marines earlier in 1944.

I had had a long discussion with Mac McKirgen about a way to get the dogs off of the ship without going down a cargo net—and taking over an hour of valuable landing time. Mac figured that if we split the dogs and men into four groups, we could have the boats come to the railing on the deck, load the men and dogs and lower the boats to the water. At Kwajalein, we were taken to one of the little islands for recreation, and as decided, the boats were lifted to the gunwale, the men and dogs loaded, the boats lowered to the water and we were on our way in ten minutes. I looked up to the bridge, and with a huge grin the captain gave me a victory salute.

The little island was only a hundred yards across and about five hundred yards long, with the highest point just a few feet above sea level. It was a beautiful islet with coral sand so inviting that when the boats grounded, the men and dogs sloshed through the shallow water and ran ashore. Across the island, the ocean crashed across a reef. There were small coconut palms, which provided some shade from the tropical sun, and some low vines; otherwise there was no foliage.

The men swam in the warm water, the dogs waded into retrieve balls or pieces of driftwood and then swam back to their handlers on the shore when the sun became hot, and the game of gathering coconuts and having the dogs tear off the husks began. The boats remained with us throughout the morning, carrying men out into the lagoon for diving. The crews provided snorkels and masks, and we floated around exploring the water and the ocean floor. The water was more than two hundred feet deep, and when viewed through a mask, every particle of sea life was as clearly visible as if it were only a few feet away.

The ocean floor was covered with giant clams, some more than two feet wide. In a movie I had seen about the South Seas, a diver got his foot caught in one and almost drowned before Jon Hall, a famous actor of the day, dove down and freed him by cutting the large abductor muscle that held the clam shut. Looking at those giant clams, there was no doubt in my mind that if my foot got caught in one of them I was a goner.

★　★　★

Several days after resuming our voyage to Guam, word filtered back through the crew of the accompanying ships that a terrible battle was raging. The 5th Amphibious Corps, which consisted of 535 ships and 127,000 troops of the 2nd and 4th Marine Divisions and the 27th Army Division, left Kwajalein on the June 6, 1944. The 3rd Marine Division, the 1st Provisional Marine Brigade and the Army 77th (Statue of Liberty) Infantry Division, surrounded by the Fifth Fleet of the United States Navy, and led by the mighty Task Force 58, followed as a reserve force with us attached. From the *Aquarius* toward the rear of the convoy, we could see seven aircraft carriers of Task Force 58. At first light every day their fighter airplanes departed for the Philippine Sea, searching several hundred miles to the front of the foremost ships. Meanwhile, their bombers and torpedo bombers struck the harbors and airfields of Saipan, Guam and Rota.

Late every afternoon, all hands not on duty gathered on deck to watch as the carriers turned into the wind, took their planes aboard one by one and then returned to their position in the convoy. By the third day, each carrier could be identified and the number of planes that took off from its deck counted. In the afternoon the counting and waiting took place again until all were back aboard.

Battleships and planes of Task Force 58 kept up a constant bombardment of Saipan for days prior to the invasion. On June 15, the 2nd and 4th Marine Divisions and the 27th Infantry Division hit Saipan. The 4th Marine Division later hit Tinian, the flat island adjacent to Saipan. Although the landing on Saipan was successful, resistance stiffened, and the battle bogged down.

The troop ships of the reserve force moved close to shore at night in case they would have to land reserve forces in the morning. At night we got so close to Saipan that we could see the sky light up from exploding shells and the eerie illumination of star shells as they floated to earth in their little parachutes. Before daylight the ships headed out to sea to the northeast again, safely away from Saipan and the possibility of the arrival of the Japanese fleet.

On the evening of the June 19 we watched as the planes returned from their daily mission, counting, as always. This time, a few of the planes did not return. On the morning of the twentieth the planes took off as usual, and again in the afternoon we gathered on deck to watch the planes return. We waited well past the usual time and no planes returned. Then, just as night began to fall, one lone plane came barreling down the convoy barely above the water. Its carrier slowly turned into the wind. The plane crawled up to it and landed on its flight deck. Apparently expecting no other planes, the carrier turned in the darkness and took up its assigned position. The next morning, only the one plane could be seen on deck. The other carriers had none at all.

By noon we knew the events of the two days prior. The U.S. submarine *Cavalla*, which had been stalking the Japanese fleet in the Philippine Sea toward the Saipan beachhead, lost contact on June 17. On the nineteenth, planes of the Japanese carriers suddenly attacked Task Force 58. A great air battle ensued, resulting in the destruction of almost all of the Japanese planes by our carrier planes. The Japanese planes that shuttle-bombed our fleet using Guam and Rota to refuel found the airfields on those two islands destroyed by bombs dropped by planes from our convoy and were either unable to land or, in the case of successful crash landings, destroyed on the ground.

The whereabouts of the Japanese fleet was still unknown when our planes began their search on the morning of the twentieth. Late in the afternoon, at the end of their search, the Japanese fleet was spotted, and the decision made to attack. It was known that the increased amount of fuel expended in an attack would leave many of our planes without enough fuel to return to their carriers. The alternative of returning to our carriers and going after the Japanese fleet the following day, however, was unacceptable because the Japanese fleet would by then be three hundred miles closer to the beachhead at Saipan—too close, it was determined.

Our attackers found the Japanese carriers without planes to defend their fleet, and all of their carriers were sunk or damaged, and several Japanese battleships, many cruisers and destroyers were sunk or set afire as well. Our planes ran out of fuel all along the hundred-

or-so-mile stretch of the convoy and ditched in the water near destroyers, cruisers, PC boats and submarines on the surface. At nightfall, the war ships of the fleet turned on all lights and continued to pick up survivors from the water throughout the night. We lost more than 600 planes in the battle but managed to rescue all but 119 fliers and crew. The Japanese lost most of their trained pilots, which they were never able to replace. The pilots of Admiral Marc Mitscher's Task Force 58 named the battle the "Marianas Turkey Shoot." Officially, it was recorded as the Battle of the Philippine Sea.

Several days later, when the battle for Saipan was under control, the landing forces designated for the Guam invasion returned to Enewetok. All of the planes lost in the battle had to be replaced from Hawaii and the U.S. before the landing on Guam could be attempted. Fighting ships had to be replenished with shells, torpedoes and other ordnance. The troop ships and supporting ships had to be resupplied with enough food, water and other necessities to sustain the voyage to Guam and support the beachhead once it was established.

Upon entering the lagoon at Enewetok, the odor of deteriorating bodies permeated the air, the first such smell I had ever encountered. In the short time since the battle for the atoll only a few months earlier, the low-lying sand of the atoll could not absorb the bodies of all the enemy soldiers buried there. The water table was so high that some bodies actually floated out of their graves.

We were taken to a small islet for the day, but the boats left us and would return after their day's work, loading ships. As soon as we were dumped ashore, I noticed that this island had no trees or brush that would shade us and the dogs from the tropical sun. By 10 A.M., all of the water in our canteens was used. A hole was dug in the center of the island but the water found was salty. The men took their dogs in the water to keep them as cool as possible but in spite of it they began to drink the salt water. A tropical storm brought heavy rain and the men took off their dungaree jackets and wrung the salt out as the rain came down in torrents. Helmets were set in the sand to catch all the water possible and they squeezed the fresh water from their jackets until the dogs thirst had been satiated and then drank themselves. But by noon the dogs were attempting to drink sea water again and panting so hard that I knew that if we had to stay here another few hours, I would lose them all from dehydration and heat stroke.

There was another island about a mile away and I could see palm trees. The only solution we had was to wade and swim to that island—we had no choice. The first few hundred yards we could feel the sand under our feet—then we swam. The men tried to keep the dogs from drinking sea water, but it was impossible. About halfway over, the tide came in between the islands and literally pushed us toward our destination. We found that the trees had no coconuts but, fortunately, the shells of the harvested coconuts lay all over the ground and those that were upright were full of fresh water from the rainstorm. The men filled their helmets and squeezed water from their sleeves into the dogs' mouths to keep them from loading their stomachs and vomiting as much or more than they drank. In an hour the crisis was over for all of the dogs except Tam. He had taken in a lot of salt water and was coughing constantly. I was afraid that he had inhaled some into his lungs. We lay in the shade until we were rescued by our boats. Not seeing us on the original island, the coxswains figured they would find us here. They had the audacity to ask how we had enjoyed our day.

When the mail came on Enewetok, I had been promoted to first lieutenant, and I bought some silver bars in the ship's store. I wondered if the men would feel better now that they had a first lieutenant—instead of a "shave tail," or "ninety-day wonder"—as their commanding officer.

The following day we weighed anchor and again headed for Guam, led by Task Force 53, the Southern Task Force.

★   ★   ★

On the night of July 20, 1944, we were close enough to Guam to see and hear the explosions of the 16-inch shells of the battleships as they crashed on the landing beaches. Fires set by the bombardment flamed hundreds of feet in the air. Something about the crash of the shells, the smell of the smoke, and the thought of the impending battle made it all very difficult to watch. I went to the wardroom and joined the nightly poker game, and quickly won quite a lot. Mac McKirgen was a great poker player and an expert at bluffing the Coast Guard officers, but on July 20, 1944, I outdid him. We shook hands all around in case we did not see each other in the morning and wished each other luck in the battle ahead.

Back in my stateroom I looked at the bills I had won, hundreds, with the word "Hawaii" printed on their faces. These bills, used in the Pacific, were so printed because they would be worthless in the hands of the Japanese. Money of course was unimportant; there was nothing to buy. The end of the war seemed very distant and staying alive alone occupied our minds.

I was awakened in the morning by the ship's loudspeaker, got dressed, had a cup of coffee and toyed with some bacon and eggs. I knew that I should eat something but could muster no appetite. I returned to my stateroom, got my pack and my carbine and headed for the deck where the men had already gathered. The ship's intercom barked: "Now here this. This is your commanding general, Allen Turnage. At 0600 we will invade the Island of Guam. We have been long waiting for this moment. We have trained well and are prepared."

He continued for several minutes, pepping up his troops for landing on the hostile beach: "We have the special responsibility and privilege of recapturing the first American soil in this war. Today we will liberate the first American citizens from the yoke of tyranny imposed upon them by the Empire of Japan. I expect every one of you in the Third Marine Division to do his best to destroy the enemy defenders and grant each Japanese soldier his wish to join his ancestors. That is all. Good luck and good hunting."

From the shoreward side of the ship, the outline of the center of the island could be seen in the early dawn. The naval bombardment that had continued during the night now increased to a crescendo.

Ski approached me and said that Tam, who alone had suffered terribly from the trip from Guadalcanal to Guam, had died during the night and wanted to know what should be done with him. Wrap him in a shelter half, I said, and ask the bo's'n for some weight.

I again privately cursed whoever had decided to send poor Tam overseas. There were plenty of places in the States where the Collie could have served and served admirably. I had done what I could for him, but it just wasn't enough.

Just off the beach at Asan, while planes of the Navy and Marine Corps were strafing the beaches and dive-bombing the hills beyond, we buried Tam at sea. While Pfc. Edgar Huffman, from Trenton, New Jersey, our self-appointed dog chaplain, said a few words of prayer for Tam and the dogs that we knew would follow him, dive-bombers peeled off, one after another, and dove on their objectives.

There were hundreds of them, painstakingly taking their turns. The division had been promised air superiority and we were getting it; there were no Japanese planes left.

Small puffs of smoke from antiaircraft fire on the island burst among our planes. One was hit and headed for the water, a trail of smoke coming from its tail. Some planes were armed with depth charges, the same type that destroyers dropped on submarines. From where I stood on deck, I could see the large drums of napalm and high explosive drop from their bellies and tumble to earth. Then the planes, lightened of their load, rolled over and made strafing passes along the beach. I followed the tracer bullets, their bright red arcs leaving the wings of the Corsairs and Hellcats and slamming into the beach.

Shells from the 16-inch guns of the battleships pounded the hill behind the beach, causing explosions that sent fire and smoke hundreds of feet into the air. Small fires burned along the entire length of the beach. To my left, destroyers were throwing shells onto the beach from close range. They roved back and forth, one firing a series of volleys followed by another firing into the same area. They were strung out from Adelup Point on the north (our left flank) to Asan Point on our right.

The 3rd Marines would land on Red Beach to the right of Adelup Point, which extended from the beach and rose sharply to a ridge that stretched several hundred yards inland, then becoming a cliff about three hundred feet high. This cliff extended for several hundred yards southward before joining the high ground behind the beach. Adelup Point separated the left flank of the landing from the town of Agana, the capital of Guam. As soon as the Marines hit the beach, the destroyers would lift their fire from all but the cliff.

The plan was for me to take the men and dogs in three landing craft and land on the right side of Red Beach. Upon landing, Sergeant Al Edwards with his men and dogs would go left to the 3rd Marines. My group would cross a road paralleling the beach, following the Asan River on our right for four to five hundred yards to the division command post. My orders were then to immediately deploy the men along the perimeter. With my field glasses I could identify our point of landing, just left of the mouth of the river.

On the extreme left of the beach in front of the city of Agana, LCIs were stationed almost on the beach. These small ships, most with ensigns or lieutenants junior grade as captains, had been converted to rocket-launching platforms. The launchers were spewing a continuous stream of fire. Their range was short and their accuracy poor, but at close range it didn't matter. They were doing a magnificent job of neutralizing Agana and securing our left flank.

A shell from a shore battery hit one of the little ships, which exploded and sank, and the battleship *Pennsylvania* roared to the support of the LCIs. She lowered her 16-inch guns and fired a broadside into the hill above Agana, silencing the shore gun. The mission accomplished, the battleship steamed back to her position outside the destroyers, and the LCIs continued their bombardment of the town unmolested.

Barnowsky was to land with the 21st Marines on Green Beach in the center; Taylor and his group would land with the 9th Marines on Blue Beach. This regiment would push inland, turn south, and eventually make contact with the 1st Provisional Brigade, landing simultaneously at Agat, about twelve miles south.

Barney joined me at the rail. I told him that his beach looked pretty good. There was a long flat area between the beach and the hills, and there probably wouldn't be much resistance when we landed. We might get some mortars and small-arms fire when we first hit the beach, however, so we should clear it fast. Our first contact with Japanese should be well inland on the approaches to the hills—by then there should be some cover.

The bullhorn bellowed, "Coxswains. Man your boats. Prepare to disembark troops! Away all boats . . . away!"

I called for the men to gather around and, sounding more calm—I hope!—than I felt, told them over the roar of the action that they knew their jobs. They were smarter, better trained and had a lot more firepower than the Japanese they would be up against. I told them not to forget to wear their helmets at all times, even when they were resting. Our helmets were heavy and bulky but a necessity—a shell could explode nearby at any time. Finally, I told them it had been an honor to have been with them since they got out of boot camp.

I knew each of the men well by now and had grown fond of them all. We shook hands all around. Which of them, I wondered, was I shaking hands with for the last time? The dogs were sitting at heel as if this was just another exercise, all the problems of training resolved. They were the best-trained dogs and handlers the Marine Corps would ever have. They would give a good accounting of themselves.

"Stand by to enter boats."

One by one, Barney's men went over the side, and the dogs sprang onto the gunwale and leaped into the bottom of the boat. Barnowsky was the last to go and I hurriedly embraced him. I wished him luck.

"Good luck to you, too." He jumped into the boat and yelled, "Lower away." I watched as the coxswain started his engines and headed for the beach. The men looked up, waved and were soon lost in the myriad of boats circling in the sea.

McKirgen came to the rail, looked toward the beach with his field glasses and saw our boats coming. He told me I had about fifteen minutes. When the boats were coming alongside, he looked at his watch, "You got five minutes."

I told Edwards to get his men over to their stations. Ski had divided the sick bay equipment and the footlockers with all the surgical stuff and parceled it out to the men who didn't have dogs. If one of them got hit, he was to pass the equipment to somebody else—we would need it.

Edwards would be in charge of the second boat. He was not to wait to for me when he got ashore; just hurry across the beach and the road. I told him to put his corporals in the rear and keep his people crossing the road. Anybody stopping on the beach was liable to die. The minute he stopped, no matter where he was, he was to have his men start digging even if he thought they would be there for only a few minutes. I patted him on the back and pushed him forward.

"Over the side . . . now," I yelled, "let's go." The men and dogs scrambled into the boats.

The boat began to sink and so did my heart. When it hit the water, the engines started and we sped away. The water was surprisingly smooth and I felt thankful. I did not want my propensity for seasickness to impair my ability to lead the men into combat.

As we approached the line of departure, I saw hundreds of landing craft heading in waves toward the beach. Amphibious tanks crawled back and forth, firing into the cliff. The heavy bombardment had lifted now and was concentrated on the ridge. We circled the command boat; a signalman waved his semaphore back and forth a couple of times and then pointed his flag directly toward the beach. Our wave of boats leaped forward.

I had told a small, mousy Coast Guard photographer that he could accompany us to the beach. He busily took pictures of the men and dogs in the boat and of me while I was sitting smugly on the cowling. He had been with the ship in four invasions, but no one had ever allowed him to accompany them in the boats during a landing; now he was tickled pink that I had allowed him to go.

There was a splash six feet off the side of the boat and an underwater explosion threw water all over me as the coxswain fought to right our craft. I fought the urge to jump into the bottom of the boat where I thought it would be safer, after looking down and seeing that all my men in the boat were looking directly back at me. I knew then that I would have to brave it out and stay put atop the cowling. To hide my expression of shock, I put the field glasses to my eyes and blindly pointed them toward the shore. Suddenly, it came to me that we were in a real war.

Red Beach came clearly into sight. A squad of Marines climbed a nose projecting from the cliff. When they had climbed almost to the top, small explosions scattered among them and men tumbled down the hill. A jeep with stretchers attached to it moved to retrieve the bodies, many of which lay on the side of the hill where they had been hit. But the puffs of smoke stopped; the attack had been repulsed. A larger body of men, possibly a platoon, passed the jeep and climbed slowly up the hill. Hand grenades from the hill began falling among them, and in twos and threes they began to fall. The remaining Marines continued to climb until they, too, were decimated. Three of the thirty or forty men that started up the hill reached a small crater on the very top and disappeared into the hole. Then I saw puffs of smoke around the hole.

The tide was in and the boat sailed across the reef and the lagoon. The coxswain ran the boat at full speed onto the sandy beach, throwing me halfway to the front of the boat, with the force of the impact. The men caught me and held me upright while the boat's engines raced to keep it steady until the coxswain could lower the ramp.

I scrambled to the front of the boat, and when the ramp was lowered, I stepped off the end of it into hip-deep water. I struggled to get my balance and moved toward the beach while the men moved slowly forward and the dogs swam at their sides. I looked toward the other two boats: Hamilton and Edwards were moving toward land and urging their men to follow. Machine-gun bullets kicked up water around us. I yelled for the sergeants to get the men and dogs moving across the road as quickly as possible.

We reached the beach, and I saw Pfc. Raymond Rosinski, one of Barnowsky's men and half of the team that handled the messenger dog Sieg, hobbling toward us between two corpsmen. His trouser leg was ripped open and I could see that his kneecap was hanging down on his shin. He had an "M" marked on his forehead indicating he had been given a shot of morphine. He did not appear to be in shock and gave me a victory sign as if to assure me he was okay. I asked him how the other men were that had landed with Barney had fared, and he told me he was the only one wounded when a mortar shell burst among them.

"I've got my ticket home," he said, mustering a smile.

I saw a major racing toward me, furiously yelling at me, the sergeants and the men to get moving off the beach or die. He was closer now. "Move your ass, Lieutenant," he yelled. A mortar exploded down the beach and machine-gun bullets kicked up sand all around his feet. He never even flinched.

Some of the men hit the deck, and encouraged by the advice of the major, I yelled for them to get up and move! I kicked one man, stuck immobile with fear, with my foot as hard as I could. He jumped up and started for the road, his dog following, oblivious to the noise of explosions and whining bullets. The Marine's helmet fell off and rolled in the sand; it was Tex Blalock. He dropped Duchess's (a Doberman I had gotten from Carl Spitz) leash and ran back to retrieve his helmet. Having been through this many times before, Duchess sat and waited as the bullets continued to splatter around them.

I yelled at him. "What the hell are you trying to do, get yourself killed?"

He grabbed his helmet and slapped it on his head, picked up Duchess's leash and ran for the road. "I was afraid you'd get on my ass about not having my helmet on, sir," he screamed as he ran past me.

I yelled for the men to follow me, that we didn't want to die there. We raced across the road and found a ditch. I heard a shell coming in and shrieked for them to take cover. The men piled into the ditch behind me. "Spread out, spread out!" I yelled as the shell hit. I looked back to see the major still standing there, unfazed, screaming at the next bunch of Marines coming in for not moving quickly enough. I told the men to dig in.

I dashed over to Edwards and told him he had cover in the ditch and to work his way slowly toward an embankment to our left. I pointed to a huge mound of dirt and rock about halfway between the beach and the cliff—the command post could only be there. He was to move carefully, keep the men down and crawl all the way if he had to, but not to stop. If the Japanese mortars zeroed in on this ditch, a lot of our men would be hurt. He started toward the 3rd Marines with the dogs and men crawling behind him.

I joined the rest of the men behind the dune. Sand was flying everywhere, and they needed no encouragement to keep digging as they had during training. One live mortar shell had outdone Gunny Holdren, Barnowsky, Taylor and me.

From my map case I removed the map of Guam that had been given to me. It had been drawn years ago and was completely useless: nothing corresponded to the earth around me. I put it back in the case and drew out an aerial photograph.

It was impossible to tell if we were in the right place or not. Asan River, shown on the photo, must be the creek on our right, but I was far from sure and did not want to stumble around out there until I knew where we were going. I beckoned to Ski to come with me.

The road turned to the right, and in order to proceed inland I had to cross it again. I jumped up and flew across the road. Ski was slow getting started and bullets kicked dirt around his feet as he dove into the ditch on the far side of the road beside me. We had about thirty yards in the open to go before we got to the creek, across several small shell holes. I told him to go to the one on the right, and I would take the left. We would wait a few seconds in each of them and come out of them at a different place than where we had gone in. Between holes we'd run like hell and forget about zigzagging. I had three holes picked out.

We ran at the same time for our respective shell holes, and I heard bullets crack over my head as I dove into the hole and saw, for the first time, dead Marines. One of them looked like he was asleep. He was lying on his side halfway up the crater without a visible mark on him, his rifle at his feet. Another appeared to have died while running: his legs were apart and one arm was stretched out before him. In his other hand he still held a box of .30-caliber machine-gun ammunition. There was a hole in his forehead, and the blood that had run out of it and onto the ground was almost black, dry and crusted. The third, an officer, lay facedown; his name was stenciled on his pack. As vivid as my memories of that day remain, I cannot, and have never been able to, recall the name spelled out in those letters, carefully stenciled in white on Marine green.

I crawled to the side of the hole nearest to the next objective. "Ski, let's go!" I jumped up and ran to the next shell hole. This time there were no shots fired at us.

"Go!" I howled as I ran for the third hole. When I got there, I saw that the river had made a left turn and now was in front of us. Ski and I almost fell atop each other sailing into it. If the men and dogs had been with us, a lot of them would have been killed or wounded getting here.

We rested until we could get our breath, the river ideal cover for two. It was about twenty feet across, but the stream, which was only a trickle, had cut into the earth until the bottom was nearly six feet below ground level in some parts. We sloshed up the stream, keeping low, occasionally crawling over or under a tree that had been washed down in a rainstorm past. After 350 yards, the stream divided and on its left fork we found the division command post.

The command post was not well situated. In front of the river was a cleared area about thirty yards wide that rose slightly until it reached a small hill, no more than twenty feet high. This was the only protection, one small hill. From its crest, the hill sloped down to a small draw where, on the far side, rose the high hills that led to the cliff that was in dispute by the 3rd Marines. The advance party of the division was huddled under a large chinaberry tree on the small flat area between the river and the hill, and on the other side of the river, rice paddies extended about one-quarter mile to Asan Point.

Colonel Barkley was there and wanted to know where my men were.

I told him they were dug in behind a sand dune and explained that the map I'd been given was so fouled up that I had thought it best to reconnoiter ahead and see if I could find a safe route for them. They couldn't move as freely as the two of us because they had their dogs on-leash.

He asked if I had taken any casualties and if the beach was still under fire.

I had had no casualties yet and yes the beach was receiving fire from the cliff in front of the 3rd Marines.

He told me to bring up my men, spread them across the length of the hill in front of the CP and have them dig in. If he could find a couple of machine guns or BARs, he would send them up, but I could not count on it. The hill was not under fire, so we should be able to dig in unmolested.

I told Ski to go back to the beach and bring up the men, and he looked at me in disbelief. Listen carefully, I told him. He was to stay in the riverbed going back, and when he got to the bridge, go under it and sneak up the ditch on the other side to the dune where the men were dug in. He would be safe all the way and could bring the men and dogs back the same way.

I watched as he took off in a burst of speed, dived into the riverbed and disappeared. Then I walked up the hill to see where I would put my defense. It would be virtually impossible to protect the CP from that location because the hill sloped forward to the jungle less than a hundred yards from the bottom of the hill. If there was an attack by the Japanese, the hill might be held, but there was no need for the enemy to attack it. The hill was shaped like a dome sitting atop the earth. All the Japanese had to do was to move around either or both sides of it and they would have us sitting on the top, surrounded, and could slaughter us at their leisure. What bright staff officer had picked this spot for a CP? I wondered. Probably one that had the same map that I was given.

There was a barbed-wire fence about twenty yards down the forward slope of the hill. I would have foxholes dug just below the crest, and if the Japanese tried to sneak in on us, the dogs would let us know before they got to the fence. Ski arrived with the men; nobody had been hurt and they had not drawn a single round of fire.

I gathered the NCOs on top of the hill, and we dug in on the forward slope of the hill to our left and put two men in each foxhole. Baldwin kept the holes about five yards apart and brought his line slightly forward so that he could keep the jungle under observation while Dentino, starting from the right, did the same. The men were to dig standing foxholes, waist-deep, and pile the dirt in front of them to make it more difficult for the Japanese to get at us. The dogs were to be tied to bushes down in the creek while the men were digging, and could lie on the dirt, once leveled, in front of the holes.

I set off with Ski to take some additional observations farther down the creek when Hamilton called my attention to some mirrorlike reflections up in the hills. The Japanese, we suspected, were watching our every move, just as I would have done if I were in their shoes. I told Hamilton that I didn't want the men worrying about what was up there; the best way to keep them alive was to keep them digging.

My guess was that the Japanese had taken off into the hills when the 21st had come through, but I wanted to look around and see our position from another angle in case the Japanese came sneaking back at night. Ski and I walked into the brush where several trails led up the hills, passing some abandoned dugouts on the way. They smelled like burned powder, probably from a grenade tossed into them by a Marine of the 21st, and in front of one lay two dead Japanese that had been hit by a flamethrower. Their bodies were naked and burned to a crisp, their external genitalia shrunken to the size of a newborn baby's. The whole area smelled, sickeningly, of half-cooked flesh and kerosene.

Ski leaned against a palm tree and began retching while I wet my handkerchief to wipe his face and hold over his nose. Whether they were ours or the enemy's, there was something horrible—unearthly, even—in the sight and smell of dead human bodies. The reconaissance, however, was productive. Through the brush ahead we could see the fields of fire the Japs had cleared to give their machine guns a clear line of sight to our position. If they came back tonight in a force of any size, we were going to have our work cut out for us.

Ski and I returned to the half-dug foxholes to find the men digging, but with no enthusiasm. I noticed that some of them had taken off their helmets and replaced them with issue dungaree caps. I explained that there were Japanese in the hills above us, waiting to fire only because they did not want to bring our planes down on them by opening up with a mortar barrage. When nightfall came and our planes could not fly, it would be a different story; we would have to be dug in properly if we were to survive the barrage that was sure to come. I told Hamilton to get the men digging rapidly. If I saw any more men without their helmets on, I was going to get somebody's stripes.

Hamilton, I said, should divide the men, leaving one of them digging in each hole and sending the other down to the creek. He should do it gradually so the Japanese would not know what we were up to. Hamilton passed the word and then headed down the hill and jumped into the river with me. As the men arrived, I told them to dig caves about five yards apart, halfway between the top and the bottom of the bank of the river facing the hill, three feet square and three feet into the bank.

"How many goddamned holes do we have to dig in one day?" groused one of the men.

"As many as the lieutenant wants you to dig," answered Hamilton. They dug. I returned to the CP while the men dug, because I wanted to apprise Colonel Barkley of the situation in front of the hill and to ask when I would get the two machine guns he had mentioned. If I put one on each side of the hill, I would have at least some chance of breaking up an attack around the hill and preventing infiltration into the CP. But Barkley was nowhere in sight, and the few people that were still in the CP were gathering up their gear. In small groups, they crossed the river and the rice paddy beyond and disappeared toward Asan Point. The last person left was an elderly colonel with a kindly face who asked me what my orders were.

I told him I was ordered to defend this position and was deploying my men across the hill. I said that I had no automatic weapons and forty-seven men with only carbines and some grenades.

He looked toward the hills for a while and then turned to me with the look, I would imagine, of a father sending his only son off to the gallows. He put one hand on my shoulder, shook my hand with the other and said, "Good luck, son." Then he pulled on his pack, crossed the river and went into the rice paddy. We were truly alone.

Now that there was no CP to defend, I no longer felt the need to leave my men on the indefensible hill. I could bring them down now, but that would entail exposure and casualties. I hoped instead that the Japanese, seeing us digging on the hill, expected us to stay there, and tonight would concentrate their fire there and not on the river. I would keep the men on the hill until near darkness, just before the

Japanese would begin their mortar attack, then pull them back to a better position.

If we were attacked on the ground in force from the jungle, we would have no chance with only carbines and grenades. I could probably hold on to the hill for a while from a better position, become surrounded and hope that someone would come to my rescue in the morning. Looking back toward the beach, I could not see a friendly soul between the road and us.

Stranded here alone, our chances were bad, so I told Dentino to take two men and go across the rice paddy in the direction that the people from the CP had headed. He was to find the division CP and Colonel Barkley and ask him what the hell we were supposed to do. Privately, I suspected that somebody had missed giving us the word. Indeed, they might have been killed before they could communicate it to us.

Dentino took off for the rice paddy in a dead run, grabbing two men from the creek as he crossed it. I watched as they exited the rice paddy on the far side, still in a dead run, and felt some confidence that Sergeant Vincent Dentino was the best.

Ski said it looked like we had gotten the dirty end of the stick again. And it did. The dog men had suffered so much at the hands of the supposedly elite troops and had won their respect the hard way. Had we lost all that we had gained? Had someone just not bothered to tell the dog men what was going on?

I looked up at the darkening sky and saw the last of the planes circle the hills, drop their loads, make a couple of strafing runs and head back to their carriers. Those pilots are going home to hot chow and clean sheets, I thought—and they deserved it after the work they had done today.

As the sun dipped over Asan Point, I saw Dentino racing back across the rice paddy and I ran to meet him. "Lieutenant, we're supposed to be with them," he gasped, out of breath. I yelled for Hamilton to get the men off the hill on the double. I told the men to leave the medical gear but take their field packs—time was short. The men scrambled down the hill, retrieving their dogs, and we crossed the river and started through the rice paddy. Darkness was coming fast now. As the last man cleared the river, the first mortar round came in, crashed and exploded between the river and the hill. I slipped and fell from the dike and landed in knee-deep water. Ski pulled me back to the path and, holding me in his arms, he asked if I was all right.

Just lost my footing, I said.

I looked back and saw the irrigation ditch full of men and yelled for them to get moving. Dentino, who knew the way, led us to the road. I walked back to the men in the ditch and screamed at them, and one by one they rose and began to run. When the last of them were moving, I started to run behind them, cajoling them from the rear. I must have turned my ankle when I fell because I stumbled, and Ski grabbed me again.

Dentino had wisely led the men through the cut to the shelter of the cliff on the south side of Asan Point. Here the men were standing and waiting when I, now walking unassisted, arrived with Tomaszewski.

It was, said Dentino, only two hundred yards farther.

On this side of the point it still was not completely dark. I told the men to take a break, and the smoking lamp, lit to show soldiers that it was safe to show light in combat, was lit. Then, when it was almost dark, Dentino took us to the CP.

Ski came to my side. "Lieutenant, I'll carry your pack. You've had yourself a mighty full day."

CHAPTER NINE

THE WORST DAY

Our first, interminable day on Guam finally over, we bivouacked at the new CP next to the military police company, digging, in the darkness, a few shallow slit trenches to flop down into for the night. With the exception of one panicked outburst of rifle fire in the CP, the night was completely silent.

At dawn I gathered Ski and two squads of men, and we returned to the old CP along the Asan River. The beach was still under fire as we crossed the rice paddy at double time. In front of Red Beach, the 3rd Marines were locked in a bitter struggle for Chonito Ridge and Fonte Plateau above, and flashes of light could be seen reflecting from metallic objects as enemy troops moved about in the brush above the ridge.

Some of the fiercest fighting in the Pacific war was taking place just a few hundred yards from us as men continued to attack the ridge in platoon strength. As they had done yesterday, they climbed partly up the hill before being thrown back by murderous fire from above. Machine guns from atop Fonte Plateau rained down bullets on the beachhead, and a battery of twin 40-millimeter antiaircraft guns, located on the beach, fired continuously in answer, to no avail.

The battle would continue for three more days before units of the 21st and 9th Marines assaulted the hilltop successfully from the south. The cost of taking the ridge was over a thousand casualties.

We crossed the river and I gazed in horror at what I saw. The hill and the area where we had been in position the evening before were pockmarked with shell holes made by mortars; scarcely a single foot of ground was unbroken. We gathered up the medical equipment that we had left behind and hurried back to our new CP. Now that the early morning mist had burned off of the Guam coast, I saw that it was nestled close to the south side of Asan Point along the edge of a cliff about a hundred feet high.

A short while later several of the men came to me and said that as Monty, a Doberman, was being exercised at the bottom of the cliff about a hundred feet away, he alerted to a clump of bushes. When his handler, Charlie Jones, followed up, he found a Japanese soldier asleep in a foxhole. Jones and the others had tried to awaken the soldier, without success. Approaching the sleeping man, I smelled the reason why. He was dead drunk. After checking for booby traps, the men grabbed him and pulled him upright, but he was so drunk that he couldn't hold his head up. An examination of his foxhole turned up two empty sake bottles, one empty Suntory bottle (a scotchlike Japanese whisky) and a full one for his hangover. Probably the last thing he did at some supply dump was to steal all his officers' booze and then hide as his comrades fled from the attacking Marines. If only his comrades were all so inclined.

As the men moved the Japanese soldier to the rear, a corporal approached with orders for me to see Colonel Barkley. In his tent Barkley explained that he had some work for me. Yesterday machine-gun and rifle fire coming down on the beach from on top of the cliff had endangered our beachhead. Our planes had strafed the position that appeared to be the source of the fire all day. Perhaps they had killed all the Japanese, but if there were still any up there, the general wanted them eliminated. I was to lead a patrol and eliminate any enemy soldiers that might still remain.

Gunnery Sergeant Symanski, who had chased Sandino all over Nicaragua and the Japanese all over Guadalcanal and Bougainville, would bring a squad of men and would be supported by two BAR men and a flamethrower. I was to take along a dog and handler in what would be our first real combat test of the dogs' abilities as scouts.

Whom would I take? Hobo and Bliss—about whom Gunny Holdren had said, "They sure ain't the best-looking pair I've ever seen, but ain't no Jap ever gonna get past them." Hobo was a clownish Doberman whose uncropped ears hung out from his head, giving him an off-balance, undignified appearance. But it was only a disguise, perhaps the best in all of dogdom. He was wiry and small for a Doberman, but his muscles were clearly defined across his shoulders, down his back and his hind legs. Hobo was dynamite; he could explode from what seemed to be a deep sleep more quickly than any dog I had ever seen.

In training, Gunny Holdren at first prodded Bliss to awaken Hobo as he lay asleep outside his foxhole on night maneuvers. Bliss told the Gunny not to worry; Hobo knew what was going on. As the "intruders" sneaked down the trail, Hobo would appear to be asleep. But when they got within his scent range, he would bolt upright and point his nose in the direction of the attackers.

Bliss was a nineteen-year-old, baby-faced Marine. At five feet seven or eight inches, he would never have been chosen for a recruiting poster—he looked far too benign. But he was quick, sharp, intelligent and far more capable physically than one could tell by looking at his stature alone. Together they were a good team.

Pfc. Donald Rydgig came with Hobo and Bliss and said he would like to go, too. He had his carbine hanging from his shoulder, several clips of ammunition on his belt, and two grenades hanging from his jacket pocket. He looked ready, so I said he could go, but I urged him to stay close to me.

Gunnery Sergeant Symanski was waiting with the rest of the patrol when I returned. I was surprised to see that this fierce veteran of Bougainville was forty years old, and only about five feet six and could not have weighed more than 120 pounds soaking wet. I was six feet two and weighed 185 pounds, and beside me he looked like a midget with a thin, drawn face and a long narrow nose.

He must have noticed my expression, for he told me not to worry—he could take care of any Japanese that we would meet. I apologized for staring and said that if he was ready, we would get started. I didn't see the flamethrower and asked about it.

Symanski said it had filled up with salt water when they landed and wouldn't be fixed until later in the day, and asked me how his men should conduct themselves around the dog.

Now it was my turn to reassure him: I explained that Hobo was a trained scout dog and would lead with his handler, Bliss, while the rest of the patrol fell in behind. In that formation, we headed up from the beach, where the climb to the cut was gradual. About two hundred yards inland, we came across an abandoned Japanese hospital in a cave. Cots were still there as were bedding, food and surgical supplies; it appeared that the place had not been used for several days.

The remaining climb to the road was uneventful. We descended to the cut and started to climb the ridge again. Halfway up, we came to a small flat area overlooking the beach that had been cleared of obstructing brush. Empty cartridge casings were strewn all over the ground, and two bandoleers, still containing .25-caliber rounds, were hung on a large nearby bush. From this cleared area a trail wound around to the side of the point facing the beach. Below, we could see the battle still raging; in front we faced a wall of stone that crossed the entire ridge.

The trail was only wide enough to proceed single file, so Bliss and Hobo led as we carefully made our way through jungle so dense that we could see only one or two feet into it. Twenty yards up the trail in the brush we could see light ahead.

When Hobo got to the clearing, Bliss hissed through his teeth and motioned Hobo down. Bliss crouched and advanced toward Hobo and then suddenly dropped to the ground and crawled to Hobo. He looked back at me and nervously motioned toward the clear area ahead. I crawled to him to see what he was concerned about. Across the clearing ten yards ahead, a Japanese soldier was leaning against a coconut tree asleep. To his left seven other Japanese were asleep on the ground. Two stacks of rifles were neatly standing in front of them.

My heart was pounding and my eyes felt as if they would pop out of their sockets. If we awaken these people, I thought, all hell would break loose and we would have little chance of bringing all our firepower to bear on them because the trail was so narrow.

I felt someone was breathing on me and turned, fearfully. It was the Gunny, Symanski. He looked the situation over, got to his feet and said, "Shit, Lieutenant, them Japs is dead. That dog knew it all the time."

My momentary embarrassment was quickly overshadowed by the immensity of my relief. The Gunny stepped over Hobo and me and walked nonchalantly into the clearing where, after inspecting the body sitting against the tree, he declared that they must all have been dead since the day before because they were bloated and swollen. He warned us not to get too close or touch them; they could burst at any time. Corpses left unburied in the jungle heat could pop like watermelons, spewing rotten crap twenty or thirty feet.

Our airplanes must have wounded these Japanese as they strafed the hill the previous day. They had been made as comfortable as possible and then left to die by their comrades as they abandoned the position. The men gave them a wide berth and left them to swell in peace.

The trail led on into the bushes again, but now the foliage was not as thick. After only ten yards we emerged onto a plateau extending all the way across the top of Asan Point and now were directly above division headquarters. I saw a crevasse leading down the side of the cliff that descended to just about the place where we had found the drunken Japanese soldier.

Low brush lay all along the right side. I told Bliss to take Hobo and scout out the entire area to the right and Rydgig to go through a small patch of brown sword grass near the cliff's edge just to be sure there were no enemy hiding in there.

Three shots rang out just after Rydgig entered—only two were ours. I called out to Rydgig—nothing. I called again, but there was still no answer.

I went back to the spot where he'd entered the grass and saw him prone and shaking. I studied the grass ahead of him, but saw nothing, so I lay down and crawled to him, grabbed him by his feet and pulled him out of the grass. I could see that a bullet had hit his rifle site, grazed the top of his right thumb, and pierced the edge of his right ear. I asked him if he had been hurt anywhere else. He shook his head.

The Gunny brought up his BAR men, who put their automatic rifles on their bipods and poured .30-caliber rounds into the sword grass. The bullets were only about four to six inches above the ground. After two clips had been fired off, the Gunny formed the men into a skirmish line and tossed some grenades into the grass. When they exploded, we got up and walked through the grass, rifles held at our hips, and fired into the ground in front of us. It would have been impossible to miss anybody lying in the grass, as we were only two feet apart.

We found nobody, but some dried fish and other rations near a depression in the grass indicated someone had been there. Spots of blood on the ground made a trail that led to the edge of the cliff, and there was more blood on the ground where the Japanese soldier had slid over the cliff. I asked the Gunny if we should send some men down to look for him, but he recommended that we go ahead, as we still had a long way to go. The enemy soldier was hurt, but we could not know if the wound was mortal or a mere annoyance. Symanski would bring another patrol up in the afternoon with a flamethrower and burn the patch of sword grass down. Rydgig had recovered from his shaking; he was okay. The rest of the patrol was uneventful, the ridge to the east and south clear of Japanese. We descended to the ocean, returned to headquarters and I made my report to the colonel. The Gunny believed that if the Japanese soldier was alive, he would return to his nest in the sword grass on the hill.

One of the other units had been less lucky. In a stretcher jeep, just in from the field, lay a dog that had been hit by a mortar blast. The handler, also wounded badly, refused to be evacuated until he was assured that the Marines would bring his dog to the vet.

I climbed up on the jeep. It was Allen Jacobson's dog, Kurt. Jacobson had taken a lot of shrapnel in his back and shoulders, but would be all right once he got to the hospital ship.

I looked at the big Doberman anxiously. Kurt had a wedge-shaped hole in his back about three inches wide, strangely with very little blood. The shrapnel and blast had sealed the vessels, preventing hemorrhage. Colonel Barkley told me to go take care of my dog; he would send somebody else out on patrol in the afternoon. With Ski's help I lowered Kurt to the ground.

Ski had already opened the medical gear from the footlockers and had the instruments laid out and covered with a clean cloth. They had taken several shelter halves and strung them between two coconut trees for cover. I hastily hooked up an IV bottle and inserted the needle on the end of the tube into the vein of Kurt's right foreleg. I thought about Jacobson. He had been a star halfback in high school. From the sound of it, thank God, he would not be permanently disabled.

I put a half-grain of morphine into the tube in Kurt's foreleg. He let out a big sigh, closed his eyes, and went to sleep. The explosion had done considerable damage: the top of his spine was blown off in the thoracic area, just behind his shoulders. The spinal cord was plainly visible because there was no hemorrhage at the site. The cord was glistening white and all the lateral nerves, like small white wires, were intact as they left the cord and entered the vertebrae. I recalled the time we attempted to dissect the top of the spine in an anatomy class. Our work had been crude compared to what the mortar had done. The removal of tissue was so complete that none was left to cover the wound. It might be possible, however, to burrow under some of the surrounding muscle, stretch it across the cord and then cover the whole wound with skin pulled from each side and sutured together.

I carefully inserted forceps beneath the muscle tissue and loosened it on both sides, pulling over just enough to cover the cord, and sutured it in place. While I was stitching the skin, a second lieutenant approached me.

He apologized for interrupting me, but the colonel was sending him out on patrol in a few minutes. What had happened that morning? I told him not to worry—Gunny Symanski, who had seen everything, would be with him and I would send a scout dog and handler. If the dog gave any indication that the Japanese had returned, the whole place should be burned down with a flamethrower. They should not, I emphasized, enter the sword grass themselves. The lieutenant nodded, and left with Pfc. Leon Ashton and Ginger, another Doberman, as his scouts.

I continued suturing and closed the wound on Kurt's back. Elsewhere, the dog was fine and blood loss had been minimal, but I feared that the wound would kill Kurt if the tissue over the spine swelled enough to exert pressure on the cord, or, if Kurt lived through the first phase of the operation without swelling, infection set in. In those days, we had no penicillin or other antibiotics, and an infection would be deadly. I dusted sulfa powder in the wound before I closed it. Cortisone and other steroids had not been discovered, so I had no medication to stop inflammation and swelling. I could make only primitive attempts, by today's standards of veterinary medicine, to increase Kurt's chances of survival: I added 50 percent glucose to the IV in an attempt to cause dehydration of the tissue in the area around the cord and so reduce the swelling. Afterward, I could only keep Kurt out of pain and wait for the passage of time to determine the outcome.

While I waited anxiously, a runner from Symanski's patrol returned to inform me that Ashton had been seriously wounded—perhaps killed—and his dog, Ginger, would let no one near his body. Pfc. Robert Johnson had worked Ginger for a while before she was assigned permanently to Ashton, so I sent him up alone to where

Ashton had been hit; perhaps he could get Ginger away from her master in time to save his life.

Fifteen minutes later, Johnson was back with Ginger on a leash and Ashton's helmet in his hand. It had a hole in the back big enough to stick your fist through.

Johnson explained that Ginger had alerted before she got to the patch of grass where Rydgig had been shot. Ashton told the lieutenant, but the lieutenant wasn't sure about the dog's response, so he told Ashton to get closer. Ashton walked alongside the grass and Ginger turned, growled and then started into the grass. Ashton called for Ginger to come and headed for the grass after her. Two shots had rung out and Ashton had fallen into the grass. A bullet had struck him in the throat and exited through the back of his head.

When Johnson had led Ginger away, they dragged Ashton back and burned down the patch of grass with the flamethrower and discovered that Ashton and the Japanese soldier—no more than six feet apart—had killed each other with their simultaneous shots. We had blown the Japanese man's right arm off that morning, and he had held his rifle with the stump and pulled the trigger with his left hand. Were all the Japanese as unyielding? If so, it would be a long and terrible war indeed.

I thanked Johnson and told him to secure Ginger. Then I excused myself and walked down the road until I was alone. I leaned against a tree and fought a losing battle with nausea for what seemed like hours. The loss of this fine young Marine was one I have never gotten over. Pfc. Leon Ashton was awarded the Silver Star, posthumously, a poor recompense for the years of life the nineteen-year-old had before him. Ginger would be reassigned to Pfc. Donald Rydgig, who was later killed—after our paths had diverged—on Iwo Jima. Ginger alone survived the war.

★ ★ ★

During the night, Kurt began to have convulsions from the pressure of the swollen back muscles forcing themselves against his spinal cord, so I added Nembutal to the IV to sedate him. Gradually, the dosage had to be increased in an effort to control the deadly spasms. Sixteen-inch shells were still coming in from battleships offshore and shaking the earth as they hit. To protect Kurt's fragile back from the impact, I gathered him in my arms. At 3 A.M., Kurt stopped breathing. Exhausted, I laid Kurt down and fell asleep with my head on his chest.

Major Richard Tonis woke me at daylight and said he was sorry that my dog didn't make it. I shook my head in acknowledgment and said I would have to find a place to bury him. He offered me a jeep and told me to take the dog to the graves registration detail on the beach. The dog was a Marine, by God, and he deserved to be buried in the cemetery with the rest of the Marines. Tonis would take care of everything; he asked the dog's name and said he would have a cross made just like the others. I told Ski and Quillen to wrap Kurt in a poncho and take him to the cemetery. If anyone gave them any trouble, they were to look for Major Tonis. It was the beginning of what would become Guam's Marine War Dog Cemetery.

Only later did I learn what had happened to Allen Jacobson and Kurt. They had been scouting in front of an advancing unit of the 21st Marines when Kurt alerted to a Japanese soldier in the brush. Jacobson told Kurt to stay while he snuck up to, and killed with his carbine, that Japanese soldier and another who sprang up beside him. It was then that the mortar shell had burst near them. The two Japanese soldiers had been an outpost of what turned out to be part of a much larger force, and later a battle ensued in which more than

350 Japanese were killed. According to the CO of the 3rd Battalion, 21st Marines, if Kurt had not discovered the Japanese outpost, his battalion would have stumbled into the main body of the defending force, with great losses.

After Kurt was taken away, I learned, shockingly, that Pfc. Raymond Rosinski had died aboard a hospital ship. I had seen him waiting on the beach to be evacuated with his kneecap blown off—disgusting, perhaps, but hardly fatal. Edward Topka, too, had been killed. He was found mortally wounded at daylight in a gully near the concrete bridge over the Asan River. Lucky, the big Doberman who could scale a wall more than nine feet high, was crouched nearby unharmed. Early in the night, the two of them had alerted to a group of approaching Japanese. In the ensuing firefight, Topka killed ten of them. Lucky, hovering beside Topka, growled when the corpsman came to attend Topka's wounds but allowed his master to be treated.

The instant Topka died, however, Lucky would no longer let anyone approach. Sergeant Edwards was called, and he slipped a noose over Lucky's head and led him away. Edwards remarked later that Lucky was truly a one-man dog, entirely devoted to Topka. Edwards had spent a great deal of time with them both, the only reason he was able to get near Lucky after Topka's death. Pfc. Edward Topka was decorated, posthumously, for gallantry, and Lucky was reassigned to another handler but brooded so much for Topka that the dog was returned to the States and eventually to the family that had enlisted him into the Marine Corps.

The loss of Kurt and these three excellent Marines was unacceptable to me. It was apparent that the 3rd Marines were in such close quarters with the Japanese that each knew the position of the other at all times and the dogs were not able to render the kind of help for which they were trained. I felt that the dogs, and the men who handled them, were being put at great risk and that the Marines could use them with greater profit in other ways—ways that better stressed the duties for which they were trained.

The operations officer of the 3rd Marines agreed, and the dog unit was pulled to division headquarters. I assured him that I would of course furnish him with dogs for all the situations for which their skills would be an asset. Taylor and Barnowsky came to division headquarters to confer on future deployment of the men and dogs. Together we had lost three men, with two more wounded, one severely.

The three of us had a long discussion about the deaths of Ashton and Topka and decided that until the troops using the dogs better understood their purpose and how to use them effectively, Taylor, I, or an NCO of the war dog platoons would accompany the handlers and dogs on every mission. We would see that the dogs were properly placed on night security duty and go on all patrols, to make sure that the handlers called on the troops that supported them to engage the enemy wherever possible rather than putting themselves and the dogs at risk with unnecessary heroics.

The handlers and dogs were in constant danger by being on the point position all day, every day, day after day. Once the enemy was located, the dog team was to turn over the duty of destroying the enemy position to the riflemen. The dogs were never to be used as weapons, though the men were of course to defend themselves when necessary. Our new policy was put into effect immediately, and our men and dogs were safer as a result.

★ CHAPTER TEN ★

BANZAI

The struggle for Fonte Plateau exhausted the 3rd Marines. F Company of the 9th Marines was assigned to defend Fonte Plateau, coming into the line late on the afternoon of July 25. They dug in on a defensive line and were hardly ready for the banzai attack that was about to be thrust upon them.

That night, 7,500 Japanese attacked from atop Mt. Tenjo. Late in the afternoon, the Marines on Chonito Ridge had watched them gathering in large groups and getting drunk on sake. Although the Japanese troops were far away, the Marines could hear them screaming and yelling, tossing their finished sake bottles into the air, waving their bayonets and sabers, and rousing themselves to fury for the attack they had planned. Artillery, of course, fired salvo after salvo among them, but most retreated into their foxholes and caves.

Pfc. Ed Adamski was in a forward outpost before F Company. Beginning at 10 P.M., his Doberman, Big Boy, let out a low growl. Several minutes later, Big Boy jumped straight up and pointed his nose directly toward Mt. Tenjo, the direction of the expected attack. Adamski reported to the sergeant in charge that Big Boy had caught the scent of something ahead. But Big Boy did not remain on the alert; he dropped down and curled up on the edge of the foxhole. Adamski told the sergeant that the Japanese were coming, but had stopped—for now.

Thirty minutes later, Big Boy jumped up and let out another low growl, an indication that the Japanese were on the move again. The sergeant in charge whispered to his men that nobody was to fire until he gave the word and then to fire only at a sure target. At eleven-thirty, Big Boy suddenly sprang up again, his nose pointed directly toward Mt. Tenjo, his whole body straining at his leash. Adamski grabbed him and forced him back into the foxhole, then told the sergeant that the Japanese were almost there. The attack could come at any moment.

The word was passed along the line and the sergeant again cautioned his men to hold their positions and to keep their weapons locked until he gave the order to fire. For the next thirty minutes, Adamski wrestled with Big Boy, trying to keep him down in his foxhole. The closer the enemy came to the position, the harder the job became. Big Boy's nervousness continued until the night was broken with a shriek of "Banzai"—then all hell broke loose. Big Boy let out a screeching bark at the attackers and sprang to his hind legs, straining against his leash in an effort to repel a Japanese soldier rushing toward him. Adamski fired point-blank at the man and hit him directly in the center of his chest. The handler had to grab Big Boy around the neck and fling him back into the foxhole to keep the almost hysterical dog from the enemy.

Big Boy was playing the same game he was taught during agitation exercises at Camp Lejeune and could not understand why he was supposed to lie quietly as agitators ran wildly all around him. Gradually, he succumbed to the cajoling of Adamski, but occasionally he would rise up and try to join the fray, only to be dragged down again. The tug-of-war continued throughout the night, and in this manner Adamski and Big Boy survived the onslaught.

The first wave of Japanese soldiers was cut down by machine-gun and rifle fire by Marines in the front lines. That wave was followed by a second and third wave, and then the waves became indistinguishable as the attackers melted into a screaming mob. Foxholes were overrun and those attackers not killed on the line plunged forward in a desperate effort to destroy the beachhead. The Japanese were killed by the hundreds. The ones that got through the front lines attacked the rear areas. They attacked the gunners of the 12th Marines' 105-millimeter howitzers on the beach and poked hand grenades down the muzzles of the cannons' tubes, rendering the artillery pieces useless.

All of the officers of F Company were either killed or wounded. The captain of F Company, Louis H. Wilson, Jr., wounded three times, rallied his remaining Marines throughout the night, absorbing the brunt of the assault and for his heroics was awarded the Medal of Honor. At daylight, tanks guided by a Marine who had been sent down from Fonte Plateau arrived atop the ridge and began supporting the remnants of F Company. As Marine tanks attacked, Japanese crawled onto them and tried dropping grenades down their closed hatches. They were picked off one by one by Marine riflemen.

Elsewhere along the line the story was the same: the dogs helped to give our men a critical edge. On the afternoon before the attack, Corporal Harry Brown, Pfc. Dale Fetzer and Skipper, a black Labrador retriever, had left the bivouac area and moved to the newly established front along the ridge above Asan where they were assigned to an outpost with C Company, 9th Marines. Skipper was one of the original dogs procured from the Army at Fort Robinson, Nebraska. He was aggressive when commanded to be, but naturally mild-mannered and gentle, extremely playful, like many of his breed, with an exceptionally good nose. He was one of the messenger dogs that had been assigned, with his handlers, to night security.

Harry Brown, from New Alexandria, Pennsylvania, had been promoted to corporal, leaving Dale Fetzer as Skipper's sole handler, but continued to go with Fetzer and Skipper when they were assigned to outposts at night. He had been a predental student in his second year of college when he enlisted in the Marine Corps and was a quiet, studious but extremely capable Marine. Dale Fetzer was a larger man, over six feet tall and athletically built. He was gregarious but very reliable. He had been a horse trainer in civilian life and easily transferred his skills with those animals to dog training.

Skipper alerted to the movement of the Japanese at 12:30 A.M., the front lines were put on alert and twelve minutes later the shuffling of Japanese feet could be heard before the banzai scream.

Pfc. Dale Fetzer was on his feet in hand-to-hand combat with the Japanese. In passing, a Japanese banged a hand grenade against Fetzer's helmet to set the fuse off and dropped it into the foxhole still occupied by Skipper, obediently following the command to stay under cover. The explosion sent shrapnel into Fetzer's legs, knocking him off his feet and into the foxhole on top of Skipper, already dead from massive shrapnel wounds to the upper body and head.

Corporal Harry Brown was knocked senseless, then regained consciousness and again engaged the enemy. In the morning, the battle over and all the Japanese dead, Fetzer recovered sufficiently to ask his lieutenant, Bob Dowell, to have Skipper taken to the cemetery. Fetzer wanted Dowell to nominate Skipper for a medal as well, because both men agreed that were it not for the timely warnings provided by him and the other dogs, many Marines would have been killed. This was not possible, however, because the War Department forbade the awarding of medals to animals. Fetzer gathered

Skipper in his arms and went to a nearby jeep and sat quietly until the driver came. Skipper became the second war dog to be buried in the Marine Cemetery at Asan.

★ ★ ★

At daylight, Major Tonis told me to get all the men and dogs and climb the ridge above division headquarters, where we discovered that some of the Japanese who had broken through during the night were headed in the direction of the undefended division hospital. We took up a firing line overlooking the hospital and were successful in breaking up the attack, killing all twenty-five Japanese soldiers with no loss of any of my troops. As we were armed with only carbines, I shuddered at how the battle might have turned out had we not found Transport to fix them.

The Japanese officer who had led the contingent had carried with him a samurai sword, so, in the spirit of the times—many men collected souvenirs far more macabre than a sword—I sent Ski to retrieve it and a Nambu machine gun that had opened the attack on us.

Ski also brought back to me a picture he had taken from one of the Japanese that I had killed. It showed a young soldier with what appeared to be three generations of family, and it struck me that this young man, that I did not know at all, would never again see his family. I did not regret what I had done, of course; the circumstances of war had dictated it was necessary, and in keeping the Japanese from our hospital I had saved many lives. Nevertheless, I did not feel like a hero. I gave the sword to Major Tonis.

More than 5,000 Japanese were killed in the battle of Fonte Plateau, most of their lives uselessly wasted in the ridiculous banzai attack. The following day bulldozers dug one mass grave and buried 3,800.

★　★　★

Several days after the banzai attack, four hundred Chamorros (native Guamanians) came through the Japanese lines and camped on Mt. Tenjo, and we saw firsthand another side of war. The Chamorros had been dodging the Japanese on foot since our landing and made it through the Japanese lines only because of their knowledge of the jungle. Many of them had escaped from a concentration camp, many in rags, and some half-naked. They were all undernourished, dehydrated, and sick from vitamin-deficient diets. There were infected wounds on their bodies from the torture of their captors, and others from abrasions from jungle vines and insect bites. Men who could hardly walk themselves carried others on stretchers made from poles because they had broken bones that had never been properly set.

Mothers carried small babies in their arms, the infants' skin blistered and raw from the tropical sun, which had burnt the uppermost layer and then, when it peeled, continued to burn the pink, exposed tissue underneath. The agonizing cry of the babies could be heard over the whole hillside in spite of the mothers' constantly cooing and trying to lessen their pain by having them nurse breasts that were empty of milk. Many of the younger women were pregnant.

Having accomplished their goal of getting to their American liberators, the Chamorros decided to go no farther and squatted, exhausted and hungry, on the hill. Guamanians were American citizens who had been under the yoke of the Japanese since December 8, 1942. Throughout, the Chamorros, the natives of Guam, had suffered from extreme cruelties and atrocities that had increased when the Japanese saw that the American recapture of Guam was inevitable.

The battle for Guam's liberation had continued north from Mt.

Tenjo and now was raging at places whose names would become famous, such as Tumon Bay, Barrigada, Dededo and Finegayan. All of the battalion physicians, regimental aid stations and division hospitals had their hands full taking care of wounded Marines, so division headquarters informed me that I was to take four corpsmen and all of the medical supplies that I could gather and proceed to Mt. Tenjo to render all medical assistance possible to the Chamorros until the Civil Affairs Section arrived from Pearl Harbor.

The chief pharmacist mate that the division hospital supplied was a short, baldheaded man with twenty years in the Navy Medical Corps. There was no doubt that the chief was in charge. He looked at me rather skeptically and asked if I was indeed a veterinarian. I told him that I was but that since there were no physicians available the Chamorros would have to make do with me.

The chief, fortunately, had done refugee work all over the world in his twenty years. He had brought three second-class pharmacist mates with him, good men all, one of whom had worked in the maternity ward at Pearl Harbor. For supplies we had sulfa pills, five pounds of ointments and two cases of bandages.

When we arrived, most of the Chamorros were just sitting on the ground in large groups while a few others milled around, as if looking for something to improve their plight. There was a long line leading to a water trailer where Seabees, already on the job, were distributing water in GI cans, canteens and anything that would hold liquid. Climbing out of our jeep, we were met with a loud chorus of crying children and babies. Looking at the raw flesh on their faces, the chief said his ointments wouldn't last a half-hour.

I wondered if maybe somebody knew how to make coconut oil. It might at least act as an emollient to help soothe the babies' pain while we waited for the other supplies that we would need. There were plenty of coconuts on the ridge, most knocked down to the ground by the recent artillery. Seeing the bars on my collar and cap, a sizable group of Chamorros had gathered around, and I told them that I would be their doctor for a few days until the Civil Affairs people got there from Pearl Harbor. Did anyone know how to make coconut oil?

No one replied, so I asked if they could find out from any of the older women. In a few minutes a woman about thirty-five years old came to me with an older woman in tow. It was her mother; together they had made coconut oil in her youth. If the men and boys would gather the coconuts, she believed she could do it. I listened to the old lady tell how it was done and immediately recognized the process, very similar to the way we had made lard from pork fat on my family's farm.

I would need some large steel vessels to hold the copra and a source of heat to boil off the water, and the Seabees secured two portable kerosene burners and an oil drum cut in half and washed it with solvent. In less than an hour the coconuts had been gathered, the copra extracted, and the clean oil drum halves set on rocks over the burners. The drums were filled, the burners lit under the drums, and the process of extracting coconut oil began. Maria, the elderly woman who had become my aide for the day, stood by with a huge paddle and moved from one drum to the other, constantly stirring. As the water boiled off, pure, clear coconut oil was left. The first batch rendered over five gallons, which when cooled was dispensed to the grateful mothers who began rubbing it on their babies' faces.

A miracle happened. It was as if someone gradually turned down the volume on the whole hillside. Within thirty minutes after the application of the oil to the raw faces of the children, the sound of crying lessened and quiet began to fall over the camp as the babies fell asleep, one by one, on their mothers' breasts.

But many medical problems remained. Walking through the camp with the corpsman with the obstetrical experience, it was obvious that we would soon have new babies. He could tell at a glance which births were imminent and told the women that he would help them when their time came. Then, in the midst of a tropical storm that had interrupted our first round and turned the hillside into an ocean of mud, a man came to our lean-to and asked for the corpsman: his wife was about to have a baby.

The corpsman took a jerry can of water and his sack of supplies and beckoned to me. I grabbed some shelter halves and ponchos and followed to where the man's wife lay on some dirty wet blankets that had been spread on the ground. As the corpsman examined the woman, I had the man help me stretch two shelter halves between two of the bushes. Between labored contractions, we moved her under the shelter.

I held her head and tried as best I could to assure her that everything was going to be all right. I could tell from the corpsman's coaxing that the birth was near. "It's a boy," he said matter-of-factly. Shortly thereafter I heard the cry of a newborn. From his satchel, the corpsman pulled a blanket that was miraculously dry, and covered the woman and her baby.

Before the night was over, he had delivered two more babies, all of which were as healthy as their mothers. In the morning, congratulations were rained on the makeshift obstetrical team of the corpsman and me, and mothers held up the newborns for all to see. The old Navy chief, too, grinned with pride.

By the next morning the sun was shining brightly and the soil had begun to firm up again. By ten o'clock the temperature had risen to 98 degrees, and hordes of flies had swarmed, multiplied by the dead bodies from the battle of Fonte Plateau, to attack any food that was offered to the Chamorros. To make matters worse, the refugees were depositing human waste all over the hillside.

We had to do something about the lack of toilet facilities or there would be an epidemic of mass proportions, so the Seabees agreed to requisition a bulldozer, which dug a series of slit trenches. Toilet paper brought by the dozers was hung on tent pegs every five feet.

Soon thereafter, Major Tonis arrived leading a six-by-six loaded with C rations and another truck loaded with tarpaulins. Two hours later the camp began to take on some semblance of a small tent city. Once a large tent for the sick bay was up, people lined up for treatment of wounds, scratches, sore throats, dysentery and a host of other ailments and were helped as fast as we could manage.

By evening, field kitchens were going full blast. The C rations were served hot in mess kits brought up from the division supply dump, but the flies were still having a field day. If one hand wasn't used to constantly fan your food, it would be covered with flies so quickly that there would be no point in trying to eat with the other hand. The chief suggested that we try trapping our pests and the Seabees again agreed to take time out from their other duties—such as building the airfield, scraping roads and preparing to rebuild the city of Agana—long enough to build some flytraps. True to their famous motto, We do the difficult immediately—the impossible takes a little longer, the Seabees complied, and the screen-wire flytraps were on-site before nightfall. By noon the next day the traps were full, and by the following day we had collected piles of flies three feet high to be burned. By the time the camp was moved to Agana a week later, there was hardly a fly around.

But for me it was too late. I developed dysentery, which left me with constant stomach cramps and diarrhea. From then on, I carried a bottle of paregoric in one pocket and a bottle of bismuth subnitrate in the other. In spite of taking a swig of each every few hours, I still had several loose stools a day.

The Chamorros were to be moved to a new camp in Agana, and I returned to my duties with the war dog platoons. For as long as I stayed on the island, whenever any Chamorros saw me riding down the road in a jeep, they would wave and yell "Hey, Doc," and smiles would cover their whole faces. On Fonte Plateau, our enemies had found out what the Marines could do in war and our friends had discovered what we could do in just a few moments of peace. For my actions in defending the hospital from the Japanese who had slipped past our lines, I received a Silver Star and a Purple Heart (I had suffered some largely superficial wounds). I have worn these decorations with pride on a handful of ceremonial occasions—and thought about what we were able to do for the Chamorros nearly every day of my life.

CHAPTER ELEVEN

MOPPING UP

As the Americans pushed northward across the island, Agana, a small town in those days, was bypassed. Division wanted to make certain there were no ambushes and that no Japanese had returned following the shelling during the battle on the ridge. Division asked us to work in front of the troops sent to occupy the city.

I called Dentino and told him to have three scout dogs and their handlers ready at daybreak the next morning, and with these men and dogs we joined the patrols at Adelup Point and started north. Agana was unbelievable; the whole place was blown apart. Pieces of the highest, sturdiest concrete buildings were partially standing, but everything else was completely flattened. It was difficult to believe that a city had once stood there at all and harder still to think that someone might still be alive in the rubble. Sure enough, we searched the entire city and found no Japanese. Sadly, the war was far from over.

As we were finishing up, I received a message from Bill Taylor that Poncho, the German Shepherd I had recruited from the young boy at Carl Spitz's, had been killed during the night. While on night defense in an outpost, Poncho had alerted to the approach of twenty Japanese, and in the firefight that ensued, Poncho had been hit by a grenade and killed. There were no other American deaths, but Pfc. Willard Wise, Poncho's handler, had also been hit by shrapnel. As COs, Bill Taylor and I had the duty of writing owners and loved ones of combat deaths. Because I, not Taylor, had recruited Poncho, I would have the unpleasant duty of writing to Poncho's young master, Bobby, to tell him of his dog's death.

With Agana cleared, the division's front extended from Mt. Tenjo to Agana, about five miles. For the first time in history, a Marine war dog led every point of a Marine division. Twelve dogs and handlers of the 2nd and 3d War Dog Platoons scouted in front of every advancing element of the division, and twelve messenger dogs followed to provide night security when the advance was secured for the night. Contact with the enemy had been lost after the battle of Fonte Plateau and the surviving Japanese had fled north. On the first day of the advance the airfield in the center of the island was captured (the Seabees began grading the runways before the last shots were fired). By late afternoon our Marine fighter planes landed and began close support of our men fighting on the ground.

On the second day of the advance Hobo was scouting with Pfc. Carl Bliss as the 3rd Marines advanced northward along the ocean. The two had come to a large clearing along a ridge approaching Tumon Bay. Hobo was sent out to scout the brush on the far side of the clearing and had stopped and alerted to enemy ahead when fire from the brush opened up. Hobo fell instantly. The Marines retaliated with mortar and machine-gun fire and quickly overran the small enemy outpost. Bliss ran to find that his dog had been hit in the abdomen and was bleeding profusely.

When Hobo was brought to me, I told Ski to get Bebe and a blood collection bottle. I lightly sedated her, inserted a needle into the vein on her foreleg and the vacuum in the bottle began to draw her blood into it. Bebe was a red Doberman who had gradually gone deaf, perhaps as a result of being too close to a can of TNT thrown at a demolition exercise at Lejeune. I could not use her as a messenger or scout dog so she happily became a blood donor for the other dogs.

Bliss was sitting on the back of a jeep, holding Hobo's head in his lap, when I peeled back Hobo's lips; his membranes were white as snow from loss of blood and he was in shock. There was hardly enough blood pressure in his veins to allow them to swell enough for me to insert a needle for a transfusion. Only by pumping his foot was I able to raise the vein to deliver the blood.

The bandage on Hobo's abdomen was removed, exposing the hole where the bullet had entered. On the opposite side there was a large hole where the bullet had exited his body. It had traveled from just above the rib cage on the left side to about two inches below the ribs on the right side, piercing, in all probability, Hobo's liver or spleen.

I gave him a very small amount of Nembutal; he was under complete anesthesia after I had injected 2.5 cc. (Normally, it would have taken at least 10 to 15 cc to anesthetize a dog of Hobo's size, but Hobo was weak from the shock of blood lost internally.) I washed his skin with soap and water and made an incision, several inches long, down the midline of his abdomen beginning at his solar plexus; more blood rushed out. I turned him sideways to drain as much as I could and put my hand into the incision and felt around. The bullet must have hit one of Hobo's ribs and been blunted like a "dum-dum." His spleen was pulverized; there was no way that Hobo's life could be saved. Releasing the pressure bandage around Hobo's abdomen allowed his blood to escape faster than I could replace it. Before I could find and close off the splenic artery, Hobo died.

I looked over at Bliss, who could read my expression and knew that Hobo had just died. I told him that Hobo's wounds were so severe that he had bled to death internally, and that I was truly sorry. Hobo was one of the best dogs we had, and I murmured that I—that we all—would miss him. Bliss came over and put his hand on Hobo's head: "Just like Gunny Holdren said, nobody ever got by you." He began to sob and turned away.

This was the first time the Japanese had shot one of our dogs while scouting in front of a handler, and it would become standard procedure. The Japanese seemed to have the mistaken idea that if they shot the dog, the dog would not discover their hiding place. In fact, the reverse was true. The Japanese did not always succeed in wounding or killing our dogs, but by firing their rifles, they always gave away their position.

From this point on, nothing we did prevented the Japanese from exacting a heavy toll on our dogs. The sacrifices of these dogs were recognized by every one of us that served in the 2nd and 3rd War Dog Platoons. They died; we lived.

★   ★   ★

We moved from our original bivouac and headed to Agana through the cut in Asan Point and past the rice paddy that was now the Marine Cemetery. White crosses spread out over the terrain, and graves registration people were busy digging new graves for the six-by-sixes that stood waiting to unload their cargo of dead Marines. I told the men to pick up the pace. I looked up at Chonito Ridge and Fonte Plateau, all quiet now. The artillery had left huge holes in the ground. Where the antiaircraft battery had once stood on the beach now stood all kinds of equipment and supplies, from rations to bulldozers.

We passed Adalup Point and entered Agana, still a mess. No cleaning up or removal of debris had yet taken place, and it actually looked worse than when I had last seen it, after bulldozers had cleared the streets by simply pushing all of the debris to one side. I bivouacked the troops in the San Antonio Catholic Church, which had been bombed so badly that only the walls remained intact.

In the road in front of the ruined church, I noticed in one of the ruts that someone had appeared to have dug a hole two feet in diameter and covered it up. I approached carefully and examined the soil. It was loose on the surface, and in the middle of the circle I saw a small, chrome-colored pin sticking up about an eighth of an inch above the ground: it was a buried mine. I had been taught at Quantico that the Japanese were known to plant aerial bombs on roads, but I had never known anybody who had seen one. After a careful inspection, I decided that the rest of the road was mine-free.

The sides of the road, however, were shallow drainage ditches that proved to be full of the small antipersonnel mines covered with leaves that were called tape measure mines because they looked like surveyor's tapes. I counted thirteen in just the one hundred yards of road closest to the church. These small mines, if stepped on, were capable of blowing off both legs of a man and were planted along the drainage ditches because it was common for troops on the march to walk along the shallow ditches on either side of a road, allowing motor traffic to pass in the center or to be closer to cover in case of an air attack.

I walked back to the church and called for Schaible and Butch to come and search the road, telling them that I had counted thirteen mines and I wanted to see if there were any more. Schaible told Butch to search, and Butch went to the end of his leash and slowly paced the road in front of Schaible, finding nothing except the aerial bomb that I had previously found. When he got to the intersection, however, he abruptly stopped and refused to move forward.

"There's something here," said Schaible.

I looked and could see nothing. A bulldozer had scraped the road to get rid of all the bumps and potholes made by vehicles going up the hill, but the surface was still so rough that I could not determine by observation if there was a mine or aerial bomb below the surface. But I trusted Butch.

I returned to the church, where the men had unpacked their gear, and told them to pack it back up again—we would have to move to a safer place. While the men got their things together, I located the division command post and the lieutenant colonel who had instructed me to bivouac in the church. If I didn't like the church, he said, I could bivouac the men wherever I wanted, but there were no mines there; engineers had already been over that ground and found nothing. I protested that the engineers must not have done a good job, but to no avail. Only after a jeep was blown up, with a high-ranking officer inside (he escaped with some serious wounds only), were Butch and Schaible allowed to return to search for the mines.

Now a clutch of high-ranking officers, minus the colonel who'd brushed me off that morning, watched as Schaible and Butch worked the road from one side to the other, slowly moving forward and occasionally halting to place a small flag to indicate to the Engineer Corps a mine that would later have to be cleared. Butch was soon surrounded by the brass, all very impressed with what they had seen. He did not let it go to his head. Whenever an officer got close, Schaible gave the leash a little jerk and Butch responded with a low growl and his usual grin. "Don't come any closer, sir," Schaible would say, "he's not friendly with strangers."

Later, the center of the Cross Island Road—about where all of the brass had been standing, in fact—turned out to have contained a deeply embedded bomb. The road was the main route from Agana to the east side of the island, and as such, trucks, tanks and vehicles of all types traveled it regularly. As the roadway became increasingly rutted from rain and heavy traffic, the Seabees sent a bulldozer to scrape and level it. The dozer had removed about five inches of dirt when its blade hit the fuse of an aerial bomb that was buried in the road. The bomb blew the tracks of the dozer outward and the body of the dozer sank into the ten-foot-deep hole made by the explosion. Fortunately, the heavy metal on the bottom of the dozer protected its operator from serious injury and he suffered only a concussion.

★　★　★

America was by now clearly winning the war, but the war dog platoons had sadly just begun to take some of our heaviest casualties. Pfc. Claude Sexton came to the CP early one morning and reported that Missy, our best messenger dog, was missing. She had been dispatched with Sexton to serve as night security for the 9th Marines as they marched north but had been pressed into service at the last minute as a scout dog.

We had been converting messenger dogs into scout dogs with success for some time. In the beginning, this training was done only when both handlers were present so that the dog could learn the difference between being off-leash when scouting and being off-leash when carrying a message between the two handlers. This was fine for most of the dogs, but Missy had been trained as a messenger dog for more than two years, and her genius was as a messenger. When Sexton unleashed Missy, she bolted back down Sexton's tracks in an attempt to get to her other handler, Earl Wright, who at the time was in the CP at Tumon Bay, ten miles away.

There was no trail by which to find Wright. Sexton and Missy had left from Asan Point in one of the MP jeeps when she was assigned to a forward unit, and since that time, Wright had moved with the rest of headquarters to Tumon Bay. But Missy tried anyway. She was found three days later, her body riddled with nine separate wounds and seven .25-caliber bullets, which I extracted from her body.

Needless to say, Earl Wright was devastated by Missy's death. He felt—and was justified in thinking—that had Sexton followed procedures and kept Missy on-leash, she would still be alive. Sexton felt even worse for having made the mistake. He was very close to Missy, and her loss weighed heavily on him. The entire contingent of dog handlers was saddened by the turn of events.

We were brought a black German Shepherd female that had been a guard dog at Japanese headquarters. After having an interpreter give her orders in Japanese, we found out that she had been trained for security but little else. We gave her to Earl Wright, who immediately nicknamed her "Lady" for Lady Tokyo. (Tokyo Rose, as she was called in America, never referred to herself as Tokyo Rose but always as "Lady Tokyo" on her radio show, *The Zero Hour*. She broadcast the latest and best jazz from the States, along with a sizable amount of propaganda, throughout the Pacific Theater.) After a week or two with Wright, Lady was used as a scout dog on patrols against the Japanese and proved that no nation's dogs are inherently superior to any other's, much as I might have liked to think otherwise. She worked as well—now in English—as any of our dogs. Wright and Lady went to Saipan with the 2nd War Dog Platoon and worked the jungles there, and then on to Okinawa and Japan. At the end of the war, Wright was allowed to take Lady home with him, and she gave him several litters of puppies.

Tubby's death was also very sad for the men in the war dog platoons. An obviously distraught Pfc. Guy Mason Wachstetter—always

Mason to us—awakened me at seven o'clock on a Sunday morning, angry and distraught, repeating again and again, "Tubby is dead."

Pfc. Vincent Salvaggio, Mason, and Tubby had dug their foxhole for the night, and Tubby was put in front of it as usual. Everything was quiet until about three in the morning, when they began to hear shots to their left. Tubby, sitting on the edge of the foxhole, wasn't particularly excited; they were not under attack. But suddenly there was a thud and a yip and Tubby fell back into the foxhole. A stray bullet must have hit the dog because no one heard the shot when it was fired. By the time Salvaggio picked Tubby up, he was limp and never moved again. A short time later, when it began to get light, Salvaggio saw that Tubby had been hit in his neck just above his chest.

Mason wanted to go to the cemetery to see that Tubby got buried properly, so I borrowed a jeep from Major Tonis and we headed back toward Agana. Mason was understandably fond of Tubby. They had spent forty-five days aboard the USS *Titania* before landing together on Blue Beach. On the second night on shore Tubby alerted to the Japanese, and Mason killed two who had been trying to infiltrate the CP. On the night of the banzai, too, Tubby had performed magnificently, alerting long before the attack, and Mason had killed four Japanese in front of his foxhole.

At one point the pair had gotten very low on food, and all he and Tubby had for two days were two D rations each day. (D rations were very hard chocolate bars.) Mason had to shave the chocolate bar with his K-Bar knife before Tubby would (reluctantly) eat it. One night Tubby had alerted soon before a Japanese soldier came charging into their line, yelling and screaming. Mason shot him twice in the chest and he fell down in front of the foxhole. The next morning he saw that the man had only one arm; the other had been cut or blown off several days ago, the stump infected and raw but starting to heal. What kind of people, Mason wondered, were we fighting? The man could have surrendered and would have been given good medical attention and care. Instead, he seemed to want to die; he did not even have a weapon when he made his suicidal attack.

At the cemetery I looked at Tubby's body, still unburied. He had a hole in his chest, and from the location, there was little doubt that it had penetrated the heart. There was no hole where the bullet had exited, so I was sure that he had been hit by a stray, spent bullet. Mason laid Tubby's body on his shelter half and quietly folded it over him. What a shame to lose this faithful, heroic animal by something as unlikely as a spent bullet.

As we drove back, in total silence, to Tumon Bay, the tough, six-foot Marine by my side moved only convulsively, his wet face turned away.

★   ★   ★

The tragedies that I have described were exceptions. Most of the dogs came through the war just fine, and most of those that were hurt lived to bear their scars. One dog even enjoyed the martyrdom of a heroic death without having to suffer its consequences.

While traversing Guam by jeep one day with Major Tonis, I spotted a small mass of hair and blood in the road before us. Down in a rut left by the tracks of a tank lay our little mascot Bobby. I yelled for Tonis to stop and ran to Bobby, who had been smashed almost flat. I gathered him in my arms and felt that his muddy little body was still warm.

When we got back to camp, Hamilton could hardly believe his eyes. He had just seen Bobby running around happily as he always did not more that a half-hour ago. But the impossible had happened—our little mascot, it seemed, was no more. I told Hamilton to have Ski dig a grave for Bobby under a palm tree and gather the men for an informal funeral. Mascots, unlike war dogs, I felt, should not be buried in the Marine Cemetery.

Ski made a small wooden box for a casket, and when the grave was dug, the men gathered around. Bobby was placed in the casket and lowered into the grave. "Preacher" Edgar Huffman said some prayers as I thought about what I would write to my young brother, who had so generously donated his pet to our platoons.

Then, just as we prepared to throw the first shovel of dirt into the grave, Bobby appeared. Standing on the edge of the grave, he looked down into the hole. Ivan Hamilton was the first to see him. "There's Bobby!" he exclaimed, running over to pick him up. The men jumped up and down, slapping each other on the back and tugging at Bobby, who was being squeezed in Hamilton's arms.

The dogs were exactly alike, including the short tail. The tan and white markings were on the same places except that Bobby had a small spot of tan on his right ear that was absent on the poor animal in the grave. Where this dog came from I have not the slightest idea. He must have been brought to the island by some other outfit as their mascot. I pitied the Marines who had lost this little dog: if he was as well loved by his Marines as Bobby was by the members of the war dog platoons, he was going to be sorely missed.

★ ★ ★

We moved from Tumon Bay all the way across the island to Yona (pronounced Jone-ya), the site of our permanent camp, walking the fifteen or twenty miles with all of our gear. For the first time since Guadalcanal, all of the men and dogs were together again. It was a happy reunion, of course, but it would not be long before trouble surfaced. Combat could rob us of our dogs one by one, but disease, as we had seen on the Canal, could take them all at once.

To our reunion and the war dog sick bay, Bill Taylor brought what would soon prove a useful piece of equipment. One of the caves he had explored was a Japanese hospital dump, which had contained a large store of medical supplies, including a German Zeiss microscope. It was a field unit with collapsible feet that folded snugly into a wooden case. This powerful microscope enabled me for the first time to do stool exams to check the dogs for intestinal parasites and conduct blood counts and heartworm tests.

Hookworm ova (eggs) were present in all of the dogs. Hookworms bore holes into the wall of the intestine, inject an enzyme to keep the blood from clotting and then feed on the blood of the host, be it man or dog. The loss of blood into the intestinal tract causes a severe anemia. Fortunately, I had an adequate supply of a vermicide, normal butyl chloride, in liquid form, that I mixed with mineral oil and administered by stomach tube, causing the dogs to expel hookworms by the thousands. By checking their blood counts and worming them every two weeks if necessary, I could stay on top of the infestation. Unfortunately, I was not able to do this for the dogs that were out on patrol for two weeks or more at a time. Human beings are also subject to hookworm infestation. Walking barefooted, as most of the Chamorros did, allowed the larvae to enter their bodies by boring into their feet. All Marines were cautioned not to go barefooted.

Pfc. Ben Dickerson brought Pal to me one day in his arms. When Dickerson put Pal down, the poor dog could barely stand up. Dickerson said that Pal had passed bloody stools for the past week, getting feebler each day. I looked at Pal's gums; they were snow white instead of pink, and I pricked his ear and drew some straw-colored blood into a pipette to count his red cells. Before I checked Pal's blood count, I passed a stomach tube and gave him a dose of normal butyl chloride. Meanwhile, I drew a unit of blood from Bebe, whose red blood count was kept up by giving her iron pills and worming her constantly, and transfused Pal. Within an hour, Pal sat up and ate some food, and improved daily until his blood count was normal.

Samples of the blood of native dogs (called "boonie dogs") showed, to my surprise, that they all had normal red blood counts in spite of the fact that their stools were loaded with hookworm eggs. I surmised from natives that more than half of the puppies born on the island died before they were a month old, and those that survived never had the difficulty we had with our dogs. Nature provided an immunity that allowed some dogs to overcome the infestation and live.

Because Bebe was not going to be able to furnish enough blood for all the dogs that would come in with heavy infestations of hookworms, I had Ski round up several of the boonie dogs that were running wild and kept them in our camp. I checked their red cell counts, and those with very high counts were used to transfuse our debilitated war dogs. It worked very well, and our blood supply was as limitless as the boonie dogs themselves. (The typing of blood in dogs was irregular at that time—it was known that dogs were generally not sensitive to the first transfusion but might encounter severe reactions to subsequent ones. Therefore, I used a boonie dog only once for a transfusion to each patient.)

With the microscope, the larvae of heartworms could also be checked. The technique was simple: prick the ear of a dog, get a drop of blood and spread it on a glass slide, place a cover slip over it, put the slide under the microscope and look for the microfilariae. Under low-power magnification, they appear as wiggly little wormlike creatures that kick red blood cells around on the slide if still liquid. If there was no movement, the test was negative. Under high power in the Zeiss, the actual microfilariae could be seen.

Heartworms are long thin worms that can grow to twelve inches and usually inhabit the right chambers of the heart. They can literally pack the right side of the heart to such an extent that the valves cannot function properly and the dog suffers from congestive heart failure. The dog, depending on the number of adult worms in the heart, becomes weakened, has difficulty breathing, develops dropsy (abdomen swollen with fluid) and in extreme cases dies of heart failure. Treatment consisted of daily injections of an antimony solution. The treatment mainly killed the microfilariae, preventing them from becoming adults, and it rendered the adult worms sterile. It also killed some of the adult worms that deteriorated in the bloodstream. If too many of the adults were killed at one time, however, the patient would die of toxemia. The trick was to observe the dog being treated carefully and, at the first hint of toxemia, stop the injections, give supportive treatment of calcium gluconate and infuse the dog with saline and glucose.

There is a comparable filaria that infects man and clogs up the lymphatic ducts. It produces a condition called filariasis, also called elephantiasis, so called because the clogged lymph vessels stop the flow of lymph, causing the body behind the stoppage to swell. Some of our Marines who had been stationed in Samoa in the early part of World War II became infected and suffered filariasis, called by the natives "Moo Moo." There is a classic picture, in old medical texts, of a Samoan, suffering from elephantiasis, whose penis is so large from backed-up lymph that he pushes it around in a wheelbarrow and walks along behind.

Much to my surprise, more than 80 percent of our dogs tested positive for heartworms. These dogs had not been tested since Camp Lejeune, North Carolina, fourteen months ago and it takes as long as one year after initial introduction of the microfilariae into the bloodstream before they become adults and produce the microfilariae in quantities large enough to be detected in microscopic examinations.

Microfilariae produced from the adult worms in the dog are picked up by feeding mosquitoes and live part of their life cycles in the mosquito and are reintroduced into the dog at the mosquitoes' next feeding. Then and only then can they grow to adult worms and be able to reproduce. Because of the terrible placement of the War Dog Training School, on the banks of the New River, most of the dogs became infected. Had the school been placed at Camp Pendleton, California, where there are few mosquitoes, our problem would not have existed. Instead, I treated 440 of our war dogs for heartworm in 1945 and 1946 before they could be returned to their owners after the war.

For some dogs, even the most aggressive treatment that I could provide was not enough. By the time we got to Yona, little Bunkie, the small German Shepherd handled by Art Spielman and Tex Harper, exhibited all of the symptoms of heartworm infestation. Listening with a stethoscope indicated that his heart was packed with worms. Bunkie was unable to perform war dog functions, even on night security, due to shortness of breath and lack of stamina. A test of his blood showed that it was literally swarming with microfilariae.

I started treatment immediately. Bunkie, one of the original Army dogs, was older than most of the Dobermans; I was afraid that the infestation was so great that his body could not tolerate the daily injections of antimony into his bloodstream. My fears were realized when Bunkie went into shock following the fourth injection. I stopped the injection, treated him for shock and he recovered. At that point I had the painful job of telling Spielman and Harper that there was no way Bunkie could survive the treatment—he would die a slow and painful death if I tried to treat him again. There was only one humane decision that could be made: Bunkie would have to be put to sleep.

After I told them, Spielman and Harper sat on a crate in the sick bay and talked with Bunkie for a while. "Guess it's time to go, Tex," said Spielman finally, and handed Bunkie to Ski.

Afterward, I conducted an antopsy at the naval hospital at Agana, which confirmed that Bunkie would indeed have died painfully if I had not intervened. The right chambers of his heart contained hundreds of the threadlike worms, the full-grown ones measuring eleven to thirteen inches. The Navy physicians were amazed the heart could be full of so many parasites and still furnish enough blood to sustain life. I told them to brush up on their parasitology: the natives were also infested with hookworms and ascarids (roundworms). When I was on Mt. Tenjo, children threw up ascarids six inches long and some almost strangled on them. I also observed blood-tinged mucus on Chamorros' stools, which indicated hookworms and amoebic dysentery.

★   ★   ★

After caring for the other heartworm-infested dogs, I soon became very sick myself, contracting dengue fever, also called breakbone fever. It is not a parasite but a virus transmitted by mosquitoes. For sufferers, any movement of the muscles becomes extremely painful.

Sitting up or walking is almost impossible because of the pain; moving your eyeballs feels like someone is hitting you in the head with a hammer—hard. I was sent to the naval hospital along with hundreds of other similarly afflicted Marines. In a three-week period, more than 15,000 troops had come down with dengue fever. At any one time, 25 percent of the Marines of the 3rd Marine Division were debilitated with it.

If the Japanese, who I assume got dengue when they first arrived on Guam and were now immune to it, had lain back for two or three weeks and waited for dengue to strike the invaders, they could have been able to walk up to our foxholes and knock us over with sticks. The treatment was codeine for pain and Nembutal to induce sleep, and nothing else besides the body's immune system and time could help. After the first contraction, fortunately, men were thereafter immune to dengue.

I recovered from dengue fever slowly, over a period of about two weeks, and stayed on in the naval hospital for another couple of days to help the naval doctors attack the parasites that had infected the Chamorros. By this time Guam had been declared secure—meaning only that Marines in units of a company or larger could expect to overcome any residual Japanese that might be encountered. Over 8,000 Japanese, it was estimated, actually remained. The job for the war dogs and their handlers—to help to locate and capture these men—was bigger than ever.

I had put the dengue fever behind me, but the dysentery that I had had since I was up on Mt. Tenjo with the Chamorros was not getting any better. I had taken two courses of sulfaguanidine and still carried a bottle of paregoric and a bottle of bismuth in each hip pocket. I had weighed 185 pounds when I had boarded the *Skinner* in California and now was down to 123.

A culture confirmed that I had bacillary dysentery caused by a bacterium by the name of shigella in addition to amoebic dysentery. I was immediately put on sulfadiazine for the shigella and emetine, an alkaloid of ipecac used to destroy the parasitic amoeba. I took the medicine as directed and it lessened the problem while I was taking it, but when the treatment was completed, the dysentery returned, as violent as ever. I continued to go on patrols with the paregoric and bismuth.

★ ★ ★

For many months in Tumon Bay the war dog platoons had been working closely with the Military Police Company, so for practical as well as personal reasons I asked Major Tonis if the 2nd and 3rd Platoons could be attached to the Military Police Company. Major Tonis said he would be delighted and requested the transfer, which resulted in the war dog platoons staying with the MP Company for the rest of the war.

Major Tonis, to whom we would now report, had gained great respect for the work of the dogs. On several occasions the dogs had alerted to Japanese attempting to sneak up on MPs who were stationed at crossroads at night, thus saving many lives. During the mop-up of the island, now proceeding apace, dogs and handlers would be used differently. Japanese hid in the jungle and attacked isolated farmers returning to their homes, or raided supply dumps to obtain food, sometimes in squads. When spotted, they beat a fast retreat back to the jungle.

As part of the mop-up operation, patrol units were formed and sent out into the jungle to locate any enemy hiding in the bush. These units, which included a scout dog and handler, stayed out for two to three weeks at a time and then were brought back into camp and replaced by another unit. At any given time we had fifteen to twenty dogs out in the field.

On one occasion Division had reported that, shortly before daylight, cooks of the 21st Marines, bivouacked on the road leading to Cabras Island, were making morning coffee when they spotted a group of Japanese, about a squad in number, walking single file toward the causeway to the now unoccupied Cabras Island. A few minutes later the guard post on the road saw the end of the column as it disappeared onto the causeway heading to the island. They had passed the guard post undetected in the dark and only by chance were they seen at all.

The officer of the day at the 21st Marines called division headquarters and asked how to proceed. After some discussion, it was determined that because of the rocky terrain and brush, it would be suicide to send Marines alone into ground so perfectly suitable to an ambush. So Major Tonis looked at me and scowled: "Division said for you to take some of your dog people and go after them."

This was a raw deal, of course. Someone had fallen asleep on duty and let a bunch of Japanese by and so I would have to put my men at risk to remedy the situation. But Major Tonis quieted my complaints by saying that the dog men and their dogs had built up that kind of reputation during the campaign. He would send a couple of BAR men and a flamethrower with us, which would help.

Dentino gathered Butch and Keith Schaible, Cappy and Stanley Terrell, Koko and Raymond Polanski and Rusty and Walter Josefiak and we scrambled into a six-by-six along with the BAR men and the man with the flamethrower and headed to Cabras Island, where the Japanese were expected to be hiding.

The CP at Yona, on the east coast of Guam, overlooked the Bay of Pago. We drove westward over the hills in the center of the island to Agana, then south through the cut in Asan Point, where so much had happened to us before, and on to Cabras Island. Cabras Island is located about one-third of the way up the west coast of Guam and is connected with the main island by a short narrow causeway, just wide enough to permit one wheeled vehicle to cross at a time. Geographically, Cabras Island forms the north and west shoulder of Apra Harbor, at the head of a long reef that extends south from the entrance opposite Orote Point.

In the initial battle for Guam, the 9th Marines had made an amphibious landing on Cabras Island, and the Japanese who occupied it were either killed or driven off. Now, weeks later, it had to be done all over again. Marines standing around near the causeway reported to me that the Japs were shooting at them; some rounds had just come over from there.

We crossed the causeway alone.

The center of the Island was rocky and some of the rocks were huge. There was a smattering of brush here and there, but we were able to maneuver through it easily because so much of it had been destroyed by shellfire during the initial landing. Schaible and Butch lead to the left side of the rocks, Rydgig and Johnson following about ten yards behind, a little off to either side. Terrell and Cappy formed to the right with Dickerson on Terrell's left and me on the right. In a similar formation on the right side of the rocks, Voight and Dentino followed Koko and Polanski, with Rusty and Josefiak leading Spielman and Blalock. The BAR men took a position on each side of the coral rocks, the man with the flamethrower slightly behind me. If I were hit, Sergeant Dentino would be in charge.

We worked the dogs off-leash, in complete silence. Terrell gave Cappy a big hug and sent him out. When Terrell held up his arm signaling Cappy to hold, the black and tan Doberman stopped dead in his tracks. Our line was good, the other dogs also out and holding as we fanned out. The dogs moved gracefully, jumping small rocks, circumventing others, quartering and moving ahead at the arm and hand signals of their handlers.

The rocks appeared at times to be in piles, as if forming a breakwater. They were fractured and pointed and showed little signs of erosion. Up ahead as we moved forward, a large rock about fifteen or so feet tall lay sideways coming to a sharp point at the top that leaned southward, away from us, and rested on another rock. We were still fifty yards away, so I gave the sign to be alert, extending my hand in front of my eyes, palm down and pointing to the rock. I motioned for the men on either side to move in closer. If the Japanese were still on this island, I was sure they would be holed up under one of these big rocks. The skirmish line tightened.

We moved closer to forty yards, then thirty-five. Suddenly, Cappy froze. Immediately, a shot range out and Cappy was hit in the chest, with blood everywhere. He was dead before he hit the ground. Terrell made a move to go to Cappy. I lunged forward, tackled him around the waist, and pushed him down.

As I studied the rock, a Japanese sprang from behind it and made for the next rock about ten yards away. Seeing that he was unarmed, I shrieked for the men to hold their fire. He ran to the rock and disappeared behind it. Almost simultaneously, a shot came from the left side of the rock he had fled. I heard it ricochet off the rocks in front of us and whine into the air.

"Fire at will, fire at will," I ordered to the men. "Take that rock under fire from both sides." Both BAR men let loose as I let Terrell go. He leaped forward and grabbed Cappy in his arms, raced back and slid behind the rock with me. Cappy had been shot in the left chest and had a hole the size of a grapefruit in his right side where the round had emerged. Both he and Terrell were covered with blood.

The flamethrower man worked his way forward, keeping the rock in front of him and Dickerson at his side. I told Dickerson that when he got to the rock, he should drop a couple of hand grenades from the top of it. As soon as the grenades exploded, the flamethrower was to torch the ground behind the rock.

The firing continued as the two men carefully worked their way forward. They crawled from rock to rock, keeping under cover until they got to the big rock. Dickerson clawed his way to the top, pulled the pin from one grenade, and set it on the ledge. Then he quickly pulled the pin from another and set it on the ledge beside the first one. He waited for what seemed to be an eternity before he pushed them over the side. The two explosions were almost simultaneous, and a great ball of smoke and fire came from behind the rock as the flamethrower erupted. A Japanese ran from behind the rock flaming from head to foot and took only about three steps before he was mowed down.

I waited until the flames died down and gave the order to move forward. The dogs leaped into action on the orders of their handlers, and as they approached the rock, they gave no indication that anyone was still alive ahead. We found five Japanese soldiers lying in various positions, burned beyond recognition, grotesque in their death.

The other Japanese man, who had been hiding behind the small rock ahead, slowly emerged, shaking with fear, his hands above his head. He was wearing nothing more than a loincloth.

Rydgig took out a cigarette and offered it to the Japanese. As he was lighting it, a photographer appeared, who must have heard the shots and come running. He took a picture of Rydgig lighting the cigarette as Voight and Johnson looked on, and was going to take a picture of Cappy and Terrell before I refused and sent him away.

To make certain we had gotten all the Japanese, we formed again and proceeded in the same manner to where the island became a reef. Afterward, the men, myself included, looked at each other and nodded, glad to be alive.

For six weeks the island of Guam had been officially secured while pockets of Japanese still roamed about, and dangerous patrols like the one I have described were conducted, by the score, every day. The Marines continued to send out patrols to make the island safe for the Guamanians to return to their homes and ranches. We went out again and again; nevertheless, some of the natives that had returned were killed—Japanese stragglers beheaded them. The patrol work was incredibly fatiguing for the men and the dogs. Dickerson and Pal, for example, led over thirty exhausting patrols on Guam—after it was secured. Between the strain of this overwork and the heartworms, an increasingly large percentage of the dogs were incapacitated at any given time. Even mighty Pal had to retire for a few days to rest.

CHAPTER TWELVE

GOING HOME

Throughout our time on Guam I continued to go on patrols and to perform my duties as war dog veterinarian with a bottle of paregoric in one back pocket and one of bismuth subnitrate in the other. At last I reached a point at which I had to return from a patrol before it even started. Sergeant Dentino took my place and a jeep took me directly to the naval hospital at Agana, where an examination revealed that I now had an ulcerated colon. I was ordered to take the afternoon medevac plane to the naval hospital at Pearl Harbor—I did not even have time to shower or draw new fatigues. My war was over.

Ski was by now well set up in the sick bay, and with Taylor and a terrific group of noncommissioned officers, I knew the men would be just fine without me. I bid my goodbyes to the troops that I had been with so long and through so much. No officer ever had the privilege of serving with better-trained or more courageous men than the Marines that served with me, nor had any similar-sized group of men contributed more to the liberation of Guam. Lieutenant Bob Dowell, whom we had worked with at Pendleton, took my place.

By the time of my departure we had conducted more than 350 patrols in the jungles of Guam. (By war's end the number would be over 550.) Japanese were encountered on 40 percent of these patrols, resulting in the capture or killing of hundreds of enemy soldiers, over 300 by the dog handlers themselves. But after the death of Ashton, not a single dog handler was killed. Many of them were wounded, however, some several times, and the dogs, always out in front, made the greatest sacrifice.

I left Guam that afternoon on a C-47, the military version of the DC-3, and eighteen hours later we landed in Honolulu, Hawaii. When I entered Aiea Heights Naval Hospital, known as the "Cane Patch," the Navy nurse in charge took one look at me in my rotten dungarees, colored red from Guam mud, sniffed, and kept her distance. I weighed 118 pounds in my field boots and dungarees, covered with pounds of Guam mud. I was sent into the shower room and told not to bother to hang up my dungarees, just throw them on the floor. After a wonderfully long shower—my first in over two months—I was clad in a hospital robe and told I was under quarantine and was to use only the toilet with my name on it. I was contagious.

The duty nurse overcame her disgust long enough to pick up my clothes with a broomstick, walk down the hall and summarily deposit them in a trash can. I went to my cell and slept twelve hours.

At the hospital in Honolulu the doctors were successful in getting rid of my long-standing dysentery but were still faced with my ulcerated colon. Not expecting to send me back to the field anytime in the near future, they evacuated me to the States. I shipped out of Pearl Harbor on the luxury liner *Matsonia* on December 15, 1944, and before the day had passed was again afflicted with the awful seasickness that had so often plagued me. I emerged only on the morning of the fifth day, just in time to look overhead as the ship passed under the Golden Gate Bridge in San Francisco Bay. What a sight.

An Army band played me off to Oak Knoll Naval Hospital, where, after three days of tedious paperwork, I was sent to the Corona Naval Hospital near Los Angeles, a center taken over during the war by the Navy from the Norconian Country Club, one of the finest and most exclusive resorts on the West Coast. I was astounded to see the posted price of the room before the Navy took it over: $67 a day—at a time when the Biltmore Hotel in Los Angeles went for $3! The Navy let me call it home for the next four months for free.

With good food and the help of Navy doctors, kind nurses and exercise, I gradually brought my weight back to 165 pounds, my ulcerated colon healed, and I was ready to return to duty. My orders came through and despite my request to be returned to the War Dog Training School, I was ordered to the Infantry Replacement Depot, Camp Pendleton, California. Fortunately, once I arrived there, my old mentor, Lieutenant Colonel Parsons, declared that I was too valuable to be wasted in the infantry and sent me along to Camp Lejeune.

★   ★   ★

I drove to Lejeune by way of Washington, thinking hard and heavy about the reception I would receive when I reported to Captain Boyd. I wondered why he had been silent when I had requested the transfer. But in the camp all appeared as I had left it. Captain Boyd greeted me warmly and we discussed the war dog program briefly. The program as a whole had been wildly successful—General Turnage himself had said as much.

It was clear, however, that things in general were changing. Headquarters was now full of combat officers; Colonel "Chesty" Puller was the commanding officer of the Training Regiment, and the War Dog Training School was under him. I was just to do my duty and keep my mouth shut.

The 6th and 7th War Dog Platoons had joined the 5th and 4th Marine Divisions just prior to the invasion of Iwo Jima, and their dogs had explored hundreds of caves. They accounted for themselves extremely well in spite of their inexperience and the ferocity of the fighting there, and casualties were quite low. (The 3rd Platoon, now under Lieutenant Taylor, had lost 8 men killed and over 20 more wounded on Iwo Jima when they were used as replacements in rifle companies.) The 2nd Platoon under First Lieutenant Bob Dowell and now Second Lieutenant Raymond Barnowsky had 3 men killed, including Sergeant Vincent Dentino, while attempting to rescue a pilot in a crashed plane on Saipan that blew up just as they approached it. They then went with the 2nd Division to Okinawa and escaped without loss of men or dogs in spite of much patrolling among the cane fields and routing of Japanese from a myriad of caves.

When properly trained, dogs and their handlers had been a tremendous help in combat, but now that all Marine divisions had a platoon of dogs, there would be no more new platoons formed. Captain Boyd said that Taylor and I had helped to settle once and for all the issue as to whether the program was to continue, and he would like for me to lecture the men in training from time to time. (They would pay more attention, he believed, to the lectures of one who had already applied what they were learning in combat.) But Boyd surprised me by then assigning me to veterinary duties instead of to war dog training, as I had hoped.

I got my gear from the car and took it to the barracks and threw it on my old bunk. Nothing in the barracks had changed. A dartboard still hung on the opposite wall, only now it had more holes around it from darts that had missed. At the kennels I saw a familiar face looking up from a dog on the table. It was Sergeant Rip Jackson, the head kennelman. Captain Stewart, Jackson said, was down at the dog galley checking in a new shipment of meat. I knew that unless Stewart had changed, he was pulling the tenderloin out of the carcass and checking it out for his evening meal. Sure enough, Stewart soon entered holding a large round object wrapped in brown paper in his hand and said, with his lopsided grin, that he had been waiting for me.

"Let's go over to the hospital, I've got to inspect some meat," Stewart laughed.

"You haven't changed a damn bit," I said.

When we arrived at the dog hospital, I could smell the potatoes baking. Stewart salted and peppered the steaks, set the oven on broil, slammed the steaks in the oven, and made two scotches-and-water. He wondered what the school was going to do with three veterinarians (in addition to Stewart and me there was Doad Cederleaf, a veterinarian who had been serving as an artillery officer overseas and had asked to be sent to the war dogs when he was returned to the States).

I said I surely didn't know. I had expected to continue as a line officer but instead was assigned veterinary duties.

And Ski?

He was fine, and had gone on with the 2nd Platoon to Saipan.

We drank, ate, and talked for many hours, and I felt very much at home.

I met Captain Clyde Henderson the next morning. He was thirty-five years old, tall, slender and had a thin mustache. We traded experiences and both agreed that sending nervous, badly behaved dogs overseas was a waste of time and a betrayal to the handlers that would be sent out on patrol with them. Gunnery Sergeant Holdren was there, too, and asked after Bill Taylor who, I reported, was just fine. I told Holdren that were it not for him, a lot of the dog men would not be alive, and Gunny dismissed my praise with a gruff nod, as was his style.

The camp was clearly overstaffed with veterinarians: three vets for just 250 dogs. Orders came in for two of us—Stewart and Cederleaf—to go overseas. They were to be assigned to the War Dog Replacement Pool that had been set up on Guam, and I was to become chief veterinarian at the War Dog Training School.

Stewart was not enraptured with the idea of going overseas, despite my assurances that Guam was a beautiful place (now that it was safe). Captain Boyd would also be shipping out on inactive duty in the last part of July, and a Major Harold Gors would take his place. With the war dog program functioning well, Boyd could retire to his homes in Southern Pines, North Carolina; Clearwater Beach, Florida; and Harrisburg, Pennsylvania. In the final analysis Jackson H. Boyd had been a friend and supporter.

Major Gors, "Happy" as he was known in the Corps, had a constant grin on his face, was thirty-seven years old and a spitting image of Douglas Fairbanks, Jr. He was a lifetime Marine—he had been in the Marines since he was nineteen years old—and had a disposition that made him an easy man to get along with. He was first commissioned as a second lieutenant for duty with the Civilian Conservation Corps, in 1933. (CCC camps were then administered by commissioned officers of the military.) Over the next year, we would become good friends and I his executive officer.

We did not have to wait long for Captain Henderson to put in for inactive duty. The atom bomb was dropped on Hiroshima and on Nagasaki in the middle of August, and the war was finally over.

★ ★ ★

Little time was wasted in preparing for peace. Clyde Henderson, Gors and I debated what to do with the remaining dogs on duty: some of the dogs from overseas that had been sent back to the War

Dog Training School had already been euthanized without ever having been given the chance to be rehabilitated. Peppy, for example, had been destroyed after Benny Goldblatt was wounded and evacuated, though I had no doubt that a dog as intelligent as Peppy could have been quickly detrained and returned home. At Benny Goldblatt's urging, I asked why this had happened and was told that "there was not time" for any other solution. I was not satisfied with this answer, and I was determined that this would not happen again.

There simply was no good reason that most of our dogs could not be rehabilitated. Time, now that the war was over, we had plenty of. The dogs deserved the chance to respond to a program of detraining aimed at preparing them for a return to civilian life. We had promised their owners that they would be returned after the war, if possible, and I was determined to see this promise kept. My life, the lives of the handlers and the lives of hundreds of other Marines had depended on dogs like Pal, Spike, Rocky and hundreds of others. Now they needed us and I was eager to return the favor.

I said I would not sign a death certificate for one of our veteran dogs unless, after an extensive detraining program, the dog had proven incorrigible and a danger to civilian society. Henderson and Gors agreed. Now that the war was over, things were different: we had the time and we had the personnel. We would give detraining a try and we believed we would be successful.

After discussing various methods for accomplishing rehabilitation of the dogs, we agreed on a course of action. Because we were plowing new ground, we would be flexible, and if we needed to alter our training as we went along, we would do so.

What follows is an exact copy of the memorandum establishing the war dog detraining program, one of the most important documents in the long history of dogs in the United States military:

27 August 1945

SCHOOL MEMORANDUM
Re: WAR DOG DETRAINING AND SEPARATION.
NUMBER 4–1945

References: (a) Marine Corps Dispatch No. 182134.
                    (b) MTC Gen O No. 13-45, dated 24 Aug 45.

1. In accordance with reference (a) and (b) the War Dog Training School will suspend from all further Combat Training for students and dogs.

2. Effective Monday 27 August 1945, the War Dog Training School will initiate a detraining program for all Marine War Dogs so that they may be suitable for return to civilian life.

3. The War Dogs will be kenneled under the present strength into four (4) Kennel Groups and each dog not in the dog hospital will receive the training and care as set forth in the new training schedule.

4. Dog Handlers will be shifted from one (1) Group to another in order that the dogs will become familiar with several persons and instill confidence and mutual respect between man and dog: enabling the dog to again become rehabilitated for return to normal civilian life.

5. The dogs on the roster of the school will be segregated into the four (4) Kennel Groups according to their various temperamental attributes or amount of training they have received. Dogs who have an unsuitable temperament or who have received advanced agitation training will receive additional attention of the handlers under the supervision and direction of the dog trainers and their assistants.

6. When the dogs are considered to be temperamentally and physically rehabilitated for return to civilian life, the Head Trainer and the Chief Veterinarian will submit a joint report on the temperamental and physical condition of each dog to the Commanding Officer in writing, with recommendations for final disposition, for transmittal to higher authority.

7. Dogs possessing temperaments which are incorrigibly vicious, or one that cannot be fully rehabilitated with complete trust for return to civilian life after a fair course of detraining, will be so reported in writing to the Commanding Officer. State the disqualifying conditions either temperamental or physical, with recommendations for final disposition, for transmittal to higher authority.

8. The War Dog Training School thus now becomes a detraining and separation unit for all Marine War Dogs. All personnel will divert their energy and experience to a successful detraining and rehabilitation program so that the Marine War Dogs of World War II will continue to be regarded with the sincere high respect and admiration for their valorous and heroic deeds which they have contributed to the defeat of the enemy of the United Nations.

(Signed)
Harold C. Gors,
Major, USMCR,
Commanding.

The following is a summary of the distribution of all the dogs at the end of the war, just after the memo was issued and just prior to the beginning of our detraining program:

WAR DOG TRAINING SCHOOL
SCHOOLS REGIMENT, MARINE TRAINING COMMAND
CAMP LEJEUNE, NORTH CAROLINA

29 August 1945

DISTRIBUTION OF DOGS AS OF AUGUST, 1945:

SURVEY	HERE	LOCAL STATIONS	REPLACEMENT POOL
45	149	38	103

1ST PLATOON	2D PLATOON	3D PLATOON	4TH PLATOON
48	35	19	46

5TH PLATOON	6TH PLATOON	7TH PLATOON	DESTROYED
none	37	39	128

DIED	KILLED IN ACTION	MISSING IN ACTION	RETURNED TO ARMY
49	29	5	8

ARMY DOGS NOT REGISTERED HERE	RETURNED TO FORMER OWNERS
43	173

FOUND A HOME	DIED IN THE FIELD	DIED AT SEA
29	19	5

TOTAL (including all Army Dogs) 1047

WAR DOG TRAINING SCHOOL
SCHOOLS REGIMENT, MARINE TRAINING COMMAND
CAMP LEJEUNE, NORTH CAROLINA

30 August 1945

Total dogs enlisted and processed by Marine Corps - - - - - - - - - - - - - - - - 891
Total registered dogs in Marine Corps obtained from Army - - - - - - - - - - - - 96
Army dogs not registered but on duty in Marine Corps from Army - - - - - - - 60

GRAND TOTAL DOGS - - - 1047

RECAPITULATION

Dogs here on duty /including hospital, 45 survey, & rejects - - - - - - - - - - - 194
Dogs on duty Continental U.S. - 38
Dogs on duty Pacific - 327
Dogs killed in action Pacific - 29
Dogs missing in action Pacific - 5
Dogs died at sea - 5
Dogs died in the field Pacific - 19
Dogs returned to former owners /150 rejects, 23 veterans/ - - - - - - - - - - - - 173
Dogs returned to new owners /found a home/ - - - - - - - - - - - - - - - - - 29
Dogs died here - 49
Dogs returned to Army - 8
Dogs not registered by us from Army - 43
Destroyed - 128

GRAND TOTAL - - - 1047

TOTAL SHIPPED OVERSEAS - 465
TOTAL REJECTED - 295

These statistics may be dull but they are historically important. They show that of the 1,047 dogs that served in the Marine Corps in World War II, 44.41 percent served in the Pacific. Of the dogs that finished training (of the 1,047, 295 were rejects), 66 percent served in the Pacific in combat platoons or on standby to replace dogs in combat platoons.

The 295 rejected dogs demonstrate improper recruiting. Thirty-one percent of all dogs arriving at the War Dog Training School were found unfit for duty, the vast majority because they were emotionally unstable. Doberman Pinschers—although they are fine dogs and did some of our greatest work in the field—were rejected for this reason in a larger percentage than other breeds. Perhaps because they were a breed small in numbers, the demands of the Marine Corps was too great to be satisfied, and subpar dogs were taken to the school for our review. Their owners also often suffered a misguided impression that we needed mean attack dogs. Dogs that are naturally mean usually have psychological problems; they are not dependable under the stress of combat. In my years of practice since the war, I have found that Dobermans are naturally as emotionally stable as other large breeds. They are sharp, fast and very tractable, train easily and retain their training perhaps better than most breeds. They are wonderful dogs.

The Marine Corps had 559 dogs still on duty as of the end of the war. The challenge was that all had to be rehabilitated to such a degree that the civilian population would not be endangered. Major Gors wondered what we would do if we were not able to detrain all of the dogs. He understood that we had promised their return, but if some of the dogs would prove to be hazardous to the very families that enlisted them, clearly we would be compelled to reconsider. I told Gors that the dogs that were still on duty in the Pacific and in the States were the best: good, stable dogs. The difficult ones and fear biters had, by necessity, been weeded out, and dogs had not undergone agitation training since they left Camp Lejeune.

If some of the dogs were not safe to be sent home, if some of them had medical problems that would preclude their going home, if some required constant veterinary care just to survive, we would then have to notify the owners, and with their concurrence, take the necessary unpleasant step.

★ ★ ★

The weather would soon become colder, and the dogs could not be left outside on stakes and chains like they had been in the South Pacific. Gunnery Sergeant Holdren, who no longer needed to train men for combat, volunteered to supervise building chain link runs down by the river, using surplus wooden barrels as doghouses.

The detraining program took advantage of the fact that the dogs were accustomed to marching in formation with a man other than their handler beside them, so although they were mostly "one-man" dogs, they were used to having strangers about. In the detraining process, a new man entered each dog's run with its handler and the dog was brought to formation with both men. After a bit of drilling, the handler gave the leash to the new man. During rest periods both men played with the dog, and at the end of the drilling session both men returned the dog to his run. This would be repeated for several days, and as the dog got used to both men, the first handler faded from the scene.

The handlers were then changed continually until the dog would allow anyone to enter his run and take him out without exhibiting signs of stress. Then we put men in civilian clothes and petitioned for the right to borrow a few women Marines so the dogs would become adjusted to a coed environment.

Major Gors thought the idea was a lark, and it was not hard to find women Marines eager to volunteer. Fraternization during working hours, of course, was strictly forbidden, and the women were sent back to their quarters by bus each afternoon. But romance finds a way. One of our sergeants subsequently married a woman corporal and the wedding took place at the dog camp one Saturday afternoon and was conducted by the chaplain from Montford Point. Major Gors had the mess sergeant prepare a nicer than usual spread for the wedding dinner, which was held in the mess hall.

By November 1945, most of the dogs that were at Camp Lejeune at the end of the war had been successfully detrained and sent home. When handlers were changed slowly and changed several times a day, the dogs soon lost almost all their expectation of being handled by one person and responded readily to the feeding and handling of many handlers. No longer were they one-man dogs.

At this point, Lieutenant Barnowsky arrived with the 2nd War Dog Platoon from Japan and took over the detraining of the dogs, becoming, since Henderson had now left, director of dog training. He continued with the approach that had already proven successful Finally, the last of the dogs returned from Guam—there were, for the first time in many months, no Marine dogs on duty in the Pacific.

I examined the dogs as they returned and found that all of them were heavily infested with hookworms and heartworms, as expected. Before the dogs could be sent home, they would have to be treated until all the heartworm microfilariae in their bloodstream had been killed and they tested negative; but before that could be done, the hookworms had to be eliminated, which would take several weeks of treatment. By feeding the dogs fresh raw beef supplemented with iron pills, their blood counts soon returned to normal and I began the arduous task of treating them for heartworm.

I hoped that when the dogs were removed from Camp Lejeune's mosquitoes, the adult heartworms lodged in the right side of the heart would gradually die, be absorbed slowly into the bloodstream, and the dog could then live a normal life. Fortunately, most of the dogs were still young and sturdy, and able to survive a treatment that would have been fatal to older or weaker dogs. Four hundred and forty war dogs were treated successfully for heartworm in 1945 and 1946. They were also treated for other parasites and diseases they had contracted during their enlistment in the Marine Corps, and skin ailments they had picked up in the jungles of the Pacific islands. Most responded well.

Barnowsky, remembering how our dogs had been used on MP duty in San Clemente before we shipped out, suggested the dogs be taken on walks in the nearby town of Jacksonville. We would thus be able to check, under supervised conditions, whether a dog's de-training had advanced sufficiently for him to be sent home. The men, dressed in civvies, walked the dogs up and down the street in town, creating plenty of interest but no untoward incidents. People stopped and talked to the handlers, and in some cases, where the handler was sure of the dog's friendliness, he allowed civilians to pet his dog.

Many people asked if they could adopt a dog when it was ready for discharge, giving us a reserve of possible homes, necessary because in many instances owners were unlocatable, dead or unwilling to take their dogs back. Quite a few handlers—Bruce Wellington and Richard Reinauer, for instance—wrote to the original dog owners and asked to be allowed to keep their dogs because of the friendship that they had developed over the years of fighting. In most cases the owners acceded and the handlers took their dogs home with them, and in the end we had many more requests for adoption than we had dogs available.

When the dogs were healthy and detrained well enough to reenter civilian life safely, both Barnowsky and I signed the certificates required for the dog's discharge. By the fall of 1946, all of the dogs had been sent home. In the final analysis, of the 559 dogs in the Marine Corps at the end of the war, 540 were discharged to civilian life. Of the 19 that had to be destroyed, 15 were euthanized due to health reasons, and only 4 were so incorrigible in their behavior that they had to be destroyed: 0.73 percent. Of those four, three were Dobermans and one was a German Shepherd, almost the exact percentage of each breed as represented in the Marine Corps in World War II.

I had said I would never sign an unnecessary death certificate and I never did. The decision made, I have never had cause to look back.

After the war I settled in Los Angeles and began my veterinary practice. I was fortunate to be able to continue to treat many of the veteran dogs that also ended up in that area, some still with their handlers, others with their original or new civilian owners. Recognizing their contribution to the war effort, the City of Los Angeles issued, at no fee, a special license tag for the veteran dogs and a local dog food company furnished free food to them for as long as they lived.

One of our dogs was left behind in Guam. Little Bobby was nowhere to be found when the trucks came to take the platoon to the ship. He is not forgotten. He placed his mark on the boonie dogs of Guam. Many of the Guam dogs now have congenital short tails courtesy of their ancestor, the mascot of the 2nd and 3rd War Dog Platoons of the Second World War.

★ ★ ★

The men that survived also managed well for themselves after the war. Platoon Sergeant Edwards had distinguished himself on Iwo Jima by commanding nineteen dog handlers pressed into service as riflemen. Only he and two of his men escaped being killed or wounded. He went to college, got a master's degree, and spent his post-war life working for NASA. Dale Quillen went to law school and became a prominent attorney in Nashville, Tennessee. Spielman and Harper, our two biggest exponents of youthful exuberance, went on to become a bank president and a college professor, respectively.

Part of me had hoped that Ski would put his growing knowledge of dogs to use and become a veterinarian, but that was not his path. Raymond Tomaszewski married his childhood sweetheart, Irene, and had four boys, all football greats as he had wanted to be. (One even made all-state.) Ski became a supervisor of building inspectors for the city of Lorain, Ohio, living a long and happy life.

During the war, Barney—Sergeant Raymond Barnowsky—was awarded a commission and in time promoted to first lieutenant. Serving in China afterward, his knee was fractured when a tank accidentally hit him, and he was medically discharged. He died in 1993 in Las Vegas after a long career as a department manager with Lockheed Aircraft Company. Bob Dowell, Dale Quillen, Bruce Wellington and I—ex–dog men all—had the honor of acting as his pallbearers in a ceremony that included a Marine Corps Honor Guard and a twenty-one-gun salute.

Ben Dickerson and Pal also survived the war. When Pal had fully recovered from his combat infirmities, he was successfully detrained and I signed his discharge papers. He and his original sergeant-owner went home to the family that had raised both of them, and Pal, I am told, enjoyed being fawned over as a hero, which he most certainly was. Benjamin A. Dickerson III was discharged, later graduated from Virginia Polytechnic Institute, went to work for Superior Oil Company, and eventually advanced to become their senior petroleum engineer. In 1989 he died suddenly at his desk while writing a letter of intent to attend a reunion of the 2nd and 3rd War Dog Platoons that would be held in Nashville, Tennessee, that summer.

These reunions have been a source of great pleasure throughout my life, and more than once a source of great amusement as well. Among the large number of our dogs and handlers that distinguished themselves in combat, Pfc. Marvin Corff and Rocky stand out. Rocky had been one of the dogs to alert to the banzai attack of July 25, 1944, and the pair went on more than fifty patrols during the mop-up that followed, staying out over two weeks again and again. On one of these patrols, Corff had singlehandedly killed four Japanese after Rocky's alert and was awarded a Silver Star for "conspicuous gallantry . . . fighting spirit and cool courage."

When I was preparing this manuscript, I wrote to Corff in the process of checking my recollections against those of my comrades. Corff wrote back, primarily about Rocky. Rocky, he said, "was not an affectionate dog. I could horse around with him and pet him but he didn't like to be touched very much." After Corff and I discussed how he should assert hmself over Rocky, the dog's behavior changed for the better, but during combat Rocky would revert:

> When the star shells lit up the sky, I could see his eyes turn green and glaze over. He went for me, getting in a few bites before I got my arms around him and put a muzzle on him. In a few minutes, he calmed down.

We were assigned to many different units and went on many patrols. Rocky did a good job. On many missions, he alerted me to enemy movement, once saving our patrol from ambush. Rocky would seem to get battle fatigue after too many patrols. He would get that green glaze in his eyes and go after anyone who was close, which usually was me. The worst bite I ever got was when I wasn't expecting it and ended up with a festering wound in my belly and flat on my back at some forward outpost. These attacks by Rocky were of a short period and then he would act normal, as if nothing had happened. . . .

I feel that outside of the numerous bite wounds that I suffered, I was very lucky in the war. When I moved to Chicago after my discharge, I found that Rocky's owner had reclaimed him. I went to see him a few times. He was glad to see me and would obey my commands, but I felt it best not to go back to see him anymore because my visits were making it difficult for him to adjust to his new civilian life.

Why, I asked Corff, had he not told me about Rocky's behavior?

Because, he said, he could not take the chance that I would take Rocky away.

Corff went on to enroll in the University of California under the GI Bill and become a veterinarian.

Of all the men I served with, I felt closest to Bill Taylor, with whom I had made so many difficult decisions. After the war Taylor went to Yale University, graduated with a degree in civil engineering and became director of the department of highways for the State of Louisiana. We have renewed and maintained our friendship at our reunions over the years, and the relationship has been as easygoing and pleasant in peace as it was in war. I can think of no other person with whom I had so many crucial issues over which we could have disagreed—and disagreed so little.

★ ★ ★

I had met the last of the men and dogs of the 2nd and 3rd War Dog Platoons at their train when they had returned from the Pacific. Only 15 of the dogs had survived the trip to Guam and back. Twenty-five dogs had given their lives in the invasion of Guam, 1 on Saipan, and 1 on Iwo Jima. Sixteen of the 110 men in the platoons were killed in action and more than 40 others had been wounded. Only 25 of the original handlers were still present when the train rolled to a stop at the same place we had boarded in November 1943. All the rest had been killed, wounded, or evacuated.

By late fall of 1946, the war dog activities of the Marine Corps were over and the men who were left were transferred to other units or discharged. Major Gors had departed in the summer of 1946, leaving me as CO, and First Sergeant Satanowski retired when he and his wife were to have their first baby after twenty years of marriage.

At the end, only Sergeant Rip Jackson and I were left in camp. I walked down and entered the empty kennel. Jackson had his sea bag all packed, and I offered him a ride to the Navy Medical Research Unit at Hadnot Point, where he had taken a civilian job.

"Shall I lock the kennel building, sir?" he asked as we left.

"Just slam the door," I said, "They're going to let the damn thing fall down anyway."

And that is exactly what happened. Over the years, it just fell down.

EPILOGUE

The demilitarization that followed World War II was sudden and unprecedented but altogether quite necessary. Unfortunately, one of its casualties was the war dog program that we had worked so hard to build. By 1946 military brass had decided to stop recruiting dogs from the civilian population, preferring to buy and train all their dogs from a young age. The war dog program fell into chaos and the Quartermaster Corps declared that it was discontinuing forever the K-9 Corps.

In his excellent history of America's use of dogs in the military, Michael G. Lemish writes that "the military working dog program ebbs and flows with the close of one conflict or the start of a new one." Lemish is right, of course, and right, too, in his sad conclusion that "the lessons learned are not always carried to the next generation and the experiences of the past are often lost, only sometimes rediscovered, and all too often ignored." For the dogs, the most important lesson of all was forgotten entirely.

A fact sheet still used in 2000 by the Air Force titled "Military Working Dogs" claimed:

Once a dog is accepted for military duty and trained, it cannot be returned to a civilian environment. The dogs could not fully adjust from a highly structured, disciplined life to the quieter civilian environment. In addition, they could not tolerate the loss of constant companionship, exercise, and attention that had become their way of life. When they become too senile for continued duty or incurably ill, directives specify humane disposition procedures much like those practiced by civilian veterinary doctors.

Soon after the end of the Second World War, many canine behaviorists said that all military dogs had been destroyed because it was not possible to detrain dogs after military service to the extent that they would be safe for return to civilian life. The reader of this book knows differently. We brought our dogs home with us from the battlefields. Our dogs were not destroyed: they were detrained and successfully returned to civilian life. How reliable was the detraining? There was never a single case reported where one of our dogs attacked a human after returning to civilian life.

Yet for years the military persisted in a policy that was both stupid and inhumane.

★   ★   ★

In 1989, I returned to Guam and found the Marine War Dog Cemetery that we had begun in 1944 in total disrepair. It had been moved from its original location to the jungle of central Guam. I was shocked to find the little grave markers with their imprints of Dobermans' heads overturned and scattered about and the area covered with waist-high grass, weeds, and jungle vines. It was painful to see the final resting place of these gallant animals so desecrated.

These dogs had given their lives for many of us. They had saved the lives of their handlers and mine as well by their ability to locate hidden Japanese and know beforehand of a Japanese attack. They provided my men—and myself—with a sense of companionship and mission that was essential to surviving in such a desperate time.

I left the scene determined to move the War Dog Cemetery to a place where our government would maintain it in the manner that it does for all fallen warriors. It was a much larger task than I had anticipated, but after struggling against government bureaucracy for five years, the United States Navy came to the rescue and invited us to place the War Dog Cemetery on Orote Point, U.S. Naval Base, Guam. The United Doberman Club also helped, commissioning Susan Bahary to create a bronze statue of a Doberman Pinscher, representing Kurt, our first war dog that was killed in action, which rests on a granite monument that I provided inscribed with all the names of the dogs. The Marine War Dog Cemetery was rededicated at the fiftieth-anniversary celebration of Guam's liberation: July 20, 1994. Now the dogs can rest forever in the place of honor that they so rightly deserve.

The dog handlers of the Vietnam War were never given the chance that we had to detrain our dogs. For almost thirty years they have lived with the guilt and sense of betrayal that came with the orders to leave their dogs in Vietnam. Some never even had a chance to say goodbye. More than a million dollars was raised by the Vietnam War Dog Handlers Association, and on February 21, 2000, in the midst of a rainstorm, more than 200 veteran dog handlers dedicated a monument to the war dogs of all wars at March Field Air Museum in Riverside, California, as a crowd of 2,000 looked on. I could sense a feeling of closure for the teary-eyed Vietnam dog handlers as they placed flowers, bits of uniforms, personal mementos, a choke chain collar and even a small bowl of kibble at the feet of the bronze statue of a German Shepherd and his handler. One veteran handler wrote to me, "No one will ever erase this memory, ever. I am truly at peace in the sense that I know our dogs are remembered. They are running wild and free. They are now and will forever be remembered in the minds of all Americans."

Dogs do not build monuments to their dead. The memorials that stand at Orote Point, Guam, and Riverside, California, are for us, not them. Instead of being honored as they deserved, the dogs of Korea, Vietnam, and of the peacetime military in the years following that war were put to death. When their service ended, so did their lives. It was animal abuse at its worst, made more infuriating by the ludicrous claims of specialists that the dogs could not be safely detrained.

All this changed recently. On October 24, 2000, as this book was being prepared for press, the Senate passed a house bill that I had long agitated for. It permits handlers to detrain and adopt their dogs when their military usefulness has ended. Although, as I write, President Clinton has not yet signed it into law, he is expected to do so shortly. I do not know of any dogs that have yet been adopted out under the brand-new policy but, in the unlikely event that their handlers are not willing to take them, I do know of at least one ex-marine who would not be able to refuse to share his home.

ABOUT THE AUTHOR

After World War II, William W. Putney continued to practice veterinary medicine, in many cases on the very dogs with which he had served. During his long veterinary career he was President of California's Veterinary Medical Association and later awarded a distinguished life membership. For twelve years, he was a Los Angeles Commissioner of the Department of Animal Regulation. Following the 1971 Los Angeles earthquake, as Director of the American Red Cross in San Fernando Valley, Putney supervised the distribution of more than 200,000 meals per day for over two weeks to people displaced from their homes. In 1994 he removed the War Dog Cemetery from the jungles of Guam and rededicated it in its new, permanent location at Orote Point, Guam, on the fiftieth anniversary of the liberation of the island.

ACKNOWLEDGMENTS

To my wife Betsy, with love: Thanks for the support and encouragement during the more than five years that it has taken me to write this book.

To Chris Cosgrove: Your constant help with the preparation of the manuscript and belief in this project were driving forces in making its completion possible.

To my editor from The Free Press, Dan Freedberg: Thank you for your patience with me during the editing of this book. The final draft is much improved because of your expertise. It was a pleasure working with you.